P9-BAW-058

Also by Max De Pree:

Leadership Is an Art
Leadership Jazz
Dear Zoe

Leading Without Power

MAX DE PREE

Leading Without Power

Finding Hope in Serving Community

Substantial discounts on bulk quantities of Jossey-Bass books are available to corporations, professional associations, and other organizations. For details and discount information, contact the special sales department at Jossey-Bass, Inc., Publishers (415) 433-1740; Fax (800) 605-2665.

For sales outside the United States, please contact your local Simon & Schuster International Office.

Jossey-Bass Web address: http://www.josseybass.com

Manufactured in the United States of America.

Interior design by Joseph Piliero.

The epigraph by George Nelson in Chapter Eight is from George Nelson, *How to See,* Boston: Little, Brown & Company, 1977.

The lines in Chapter Thirteen from Walter Wietzke's poem "Liberty and License (Galatians 5:13)" are from Carl Frost, *Changing Forever: The Well Kept Secret of America's Leading Companies,* East Lansing: Michigan State University Press, 1996. Reprinted by permission of Walter Wietzke.

Library of Congress Cataloging-in-Publication Data

De Pree, Max.
    Leading without power : finding hope in serving community / Max De Pree. — 1st ed.
        p.   cm.
    ISBN 0–7879–1063–5 (acid-free paper)
    1. Voluntarism—United States.   2. Nonprofit organizations—United States. 3. Community development—United States. I. Title.
HN90.V64D4   1997
361.3'7—dc21   97–21017

HB Printing   10 9 8 7 6 5 4 3 2 1   FIRST EDITION

For

David Allan Hubbard

Whose life was the incarnation of the

ideas most of us pursue

• • •

Contents

Thanks

A book like this has many authors: people who discuss the ideas in seminars long before one thinks about a book. People—some creative, some critical—one works with who try out new ways of doing things, often at personal risk. People who encourage and smooth the way and make difficult problems seem easy. Most of these people are volunteers.

Esther, my wife, by the nature of our friendship is always my first audience and supportive critic. Most of our children—active volunteers as well as professionals—scrutinized the manuscript and scribbled their helpful notes and suggestions.

Thanks to Nancy and David Van Dyke, Jody and Peter Handy, Kris De Pree, and Charles De Pree.

The folks who work with my agent, Sandra Dijkstra, and especially Sandy herself, who never gives up, make the laborious process of getting a book into print as easy as possible.

A word of thanks to Frances Hesselbein, Steve Hayner, Ken Knipp, John Ortberg, and Sandy Dijkstra—all with significant experience in the nonprofit world—who invested talent and energy in studying the manuscript and providing precious feedback. Most of the advice I took.

That still leaves Clark Malcolm and me accountable for the results. Why Clark? Because Clark, my editor, and I have now finished our fourth book together, and our friendship and partnership have become so elegantly intertwined that we often honestly don't remember who did what. We are accountable together because I don't know how to finish a book without him.

Finally, thanks to my great friend and mentor David Hubbard. Before he died, he read halfway through the manuscript with approval, and his good opinion gives me great hopes that this book will be worth reading.

Holland, Michigan   Max De Pree
June 1997

Introduction

*T*his book is about the United States, a coun-
try uniquely dependent on its volunteers.
I suppose this comes partly from our history.
After all, no one ordered the Pilgrims onto the
Mayflower. No one forced the colonists west.

Throughout *Leading Without Power: Finding
Hope in Serving Community* are both overt and
subtle indications of an antithesis to our usual
ideas about power and leadership. In the world of
volunteers, the two are rarely connected. Leadership among volunteers is rather dependent in
beautiful ways on shared values and commitment,
on understood visions expressed in workable

mission statements, and on moral purpose. When people work for love, leaders help them move toward potential and service.

Today, in elementary schools, colleges, and universities, volunteer boards lead huge organizations, supported by volunteer alumni and families. In city councils, boards of public works, library boards, township and county boards, volunteers manage the infrastructure. We have almost one and a half million nonprofit organizations in our country. What would happen, do you think, if we required politicians to behave like volunteer servants?

In agencies of care—hospitals, the Salvation Army, senior citizen centers—volunteers chart the programs and do the work. In religious institutions and parachurch organizations, only the commitment of those who share beliefs and respond to their calling guarantees that the groups survive and accomplish their service. In agencies of nurture—Junior Achievement, the Girl Scouts, the Special Olympics—volunteers are at the heart of our society and become the grace notes in our American song. In national intervenors like the Red Cross and the American Heart Association are many volunteers who fight the tragic plague of AIDS and ease the heartbreak of natural disasters.

People working in not-for-profit groups grapple with the full complexity of today's society and have become indispensable to our national sense of identity. They allow no room in their work for the deceptive simplicity of a single bottom line. To me, they're clearly leading us to reach the potential our culture so urgently needs to be realized. They are demonstrating a quality of leadership and service arising from their understanding of and commitment to a common good, by which I mean a quality of life that touches everyone.

Their vision of a brisk and virtuous society brings us all health and respect and a yearning to reach for our own potential.

Nonprofit groups are places where people do realize their potential and do so continually. All of us are in the process of becoming.

Who can fathom the mysteries of human potential? I certainly can't, though I've been trying for forty years in for-profit and not-for-profit organizations, some big, some small, some effective, some struggling. The more I consider human potential and its intricacies, the more I believe that not-for-profit organizations are increasingly where people turn to fulfill themselves. In fact a friend of mine calls it an American irony that here in the United States, the home of the most effective economic system we know, so many people turn to the nonprofit world to fulfill themselves. Because I wish that more profit-making organizations could become places of realized potential, I don't especially like this turn of events, but I think it's true.

My experiences and my examples in this book come from both kinds of organizations. Profit-making groups can learn a great deal from nonprofit ones. I want to invite people in the profit-making world to consider the ideas from the nonprofit world because most of us move in both.

The future of the United States lies to a great extent in the hands of volunteers. My experience in the not-for-profit world leads me to believe that the search for potential—the search that moves many of us to work for love—is surely a matter of morality.

I have written *Leading Without Power: Finding Hope in Serving Community* in the hope that it will in some modest way help nonprofit organizations and the people in them understand leadership in a new light. Many of these organizations already are places of realized potential, places where people go to find something they miss in other kinds of organizations. Reaching our potential, as persons and groups, doesn't have so much to do with the how of our work as the why. Because reaching our potential is not so much concerned with the goals of what we do as with the kinds of persons we intend to become, this book does not deal with the nuts and bolts, the finances and tactics, of running nonprofit groups, important as those matters are.

I have two purposes in writing this risky book. First, to recognize, thank, and honor the thousands upon thousands of dedicated volunteers who reassert every day through their actions who it is they intend to be. Many of them have touched my life and the lives of my family and friends. Second, to offer some ideas and observations about our efforts to design places of realized potential.

One might call these essays musings on essential commitments. I don't know it all, and I hope that you will volunteer to finish this book with your thoughts and deeds. Though it won't take you long to read this book, it will surely take some time for you to become involved seriously in the job of creating places of realized potential. My goal is to illustrate that places of realized potential spring to life when we move personally and organizationally beyond mastery to joy.

CHAPTER ONE

Places of Realized Potential

*N*o question about it: potential is wrapped in great mystery. Like rainbows, which are really circles—we see only the upper halves, the horizon hides the rest—potential never reveals its entirety. People who volunteer to work with folks living with disabilities do their jobs and move ahead whether they have the answers or not. They learn to work expectantly and patiently with the mystery of potential. People who help homeless families do so with the earnest desire of releasing a little more hope and potential into the world. People who help the hungry, minister to the sick, comfort the unfortunate, and counsel the faithful all work in groups that live for the future expression of potential. Our best teachers and parents are much the same. Over years they learn to see the buds of potential, and they persistently and patiently work to help us make them flower.

This book is all about the commitment to potential on the part of so many people in our society. These people see potential not merely as self-fulfillment but as expressing stewardship and servanthood. The driving force in our organizations, both for-profit and not-for-profit, ought not to be goal achievement or asset management or quantifiable growth, important as these are. Rather, our society badly needs organizations and people that move relentlessly toward realizing their potential. Each chapter in this book is aimed at helping organizations become such places.

How can we look at our organizations and gain a sense of whether they are becoming places of realized potential? Well, I think some observable marks exist to guide us, characteristics I have noticed during my forty years or so of working in organizations that seemed to me to be trying their hardest to become places where persons can fulfill their promise. You will no doubt be able to add marks from your experience. Be sure to write them in the margin. (As in my other books, I have asked the publisher to leave room in the margins and between the lines so that you can own this book and improve it.)

A place of realized potential opens itself to change, to contrary opinion, to the mystery of potential, to involvement, to unsettling ideas.

I was in a group of staff people in a graduate school recently where one member asked for some help with a problem. The woman I was talking with and her team had made seven suggestions for improvement in their department's work processes but had received no response. Finally, they went to their boss and said, "Why doesn't anybody respond to our suggestions?" He said he didn't know. The team then published their suggestions on the organization's computer system. Almost like a Mayday call—seven suggestions for improvement in case anybody's interested. Still no response. It seems trivial, but it's tragic. A closed organization is a tragedy. An open one holds enormous promise.

Places of realized potential offer people the opportunity to learn and to grow. For over thirty years I've served on the board of trustees at Fuller Theological Seminary, and for me it has been one of the most effective growing experiences I've ever had. The chance to work with faculty, students, and other board members has enriched me beyond measure. The study sessions for the board have given the participants a sense of the worldwide context in which the seminary must operate. The opportunity to serve such an institution has given me and many others a chance at genuine problem ownership and a strong sense of being involved and important in the work of the institution.

One of the key reasons people work full time and volunteer for work in not-for-profit organizations is because these organizations have such high reputations for giving people the opportunity to learn and grow. This means too that it's important for the organization and its leaders to see how serious is their responsibility for good orientation and training, especially for volunteers.

A place of realized potential offers the gift of challenging work. One of the easiest mistakes is to tell people that you have a job for them, that you need them to do it, but that the job is not very hard and not much preparation is required to be successful. This is clearly not the way to offer work. We should offer challenging work. We should offer work that's difficult. We should offer work that's risky, because through risky work we grow. We should offer work that's meaningful. We should offer work that matches the gifts of the person. Easy work is as rewarding as steering a parked car.

Many years ago a woman in the church my wife, Esther, and I belonged to asked me to help in a class for high school kids who had given previous teachers fits. The woman impressed me by saying, "This is the toughest job in the church. I've agreed to do it only if you'll help." She knew how to offer challenging work, and I accepted. Next, of course, we began to prepare ourselves, because all students deserve to be taken seriously.

A place of realized potential sheds its obsolete baggage. It's a place where people understand the significance of abandonment. No one has infinite budgets or energy or other resources. If we're to take on new projects, new challenges, we must be prepared to abandon the obsolete. In the work of organizations, innovation and renewal are related to our ability to abandon the less important and the unnecessary.

A place of realized potential encourages people to decide what needs to be measured and then helps them do the work. I just want to drop a friendly word of warning: don't measure only what's easily measurable. We need to learn how to measure what's significant, how to measure matters of the spirit, how to measure strategic needs, how to measure competence, how to measure results. We also need to learn how to measure moral purpose in our organizations. In the process we need to learn to sense potential and nurture moral purpose.

Of course measurements can be put to all kinds of uses—including blameworthy ones. Working with measurements easily arrived at, especially measurements of the less important aspects of organizational life, leaves us yawning and unfulfilled. When we depend on easy measurements, we risk taking a part for the whole—thinking that because we can see only half of the rainbow that's all there is. (We'll talk more about measurements in Chapter Four.)

A place of realized potential heals people with trust and with caring and with forgetfulness. It's a place that forgives the mistakes of growing up, a place that understands that taking a risk may mean failure but that ordinarily mistakes should not be terminal.

I don't tell this story with any pride, but some time ago when I was still CEO at Herman Miller, the office furniture company where I worked for most of my life, I got a call from a salesman whom I had known for more than ten years. "I'm calling you," he said, "because we've been friends for a long time, and I just want you to know I'm going to work for the competition." This came as a real surprise because I had always thought of this man as a person with a fine future in the company. Naturally, I was interested to know why he was leaving Herman Miller. He said, "I'm leaving because I have a broken heart. I made a mistake eight years ago and nobody will forget it." Most of us at a certain point know that heartache is everywhere. Organizations that wish to reach their potential and that enable the individuals within them to reach their personal potential understand the role of healing.

People in places of realized potential know that organizations are social environments. They perceive their organizations as social entities with a role in society far beyond that of making money. As a result, these people look at the whole of life, with all its messy complications, a reality requiring us to think clearly about what's important, what comes first. We can't do everything.

Last, a place of realized potential celebrates. People there are serious about its rewards. They know how to design rewards, for they understand that the best way to reward outstanding performance is to raise the level of challenge. (Outstanding performers lose the right to occasional mediocrity.) A place that celebrates honors its stated values. A place that celebrates relentlessly identifies good models. A place that celebrates knows how to say thanks.

Esther and I have eleven grandchildren. One of them born weeks premature is now in 3rd grade, and while she has some special challenges, she is really doing quite well. One day when she was three years old, she came to visit me in my office, which is in a small condominium. She said, "Grandpa, would you like to see me run?" And I must tell you, my heart jumped. I thought to myself, this little girl can hardly walk. How is she going to run? But like a good grandparent, I said, "Yes, I'd like to see you run." She walked over to one side of the room and started to run, right across in front of my desk and directly into the side of the refrigerator. It knocked her on her back, and there she lay, spread-eagled on the floor with a big grin on her face. Like any good manager, I immediately went over with a solution. I said, "Honey, you've got to learn to stop." And she looked up at me with a big smile and said, "But, Grandpa, I'm learning to run."

Human potential remains a mystery, expressed in more ways than you or I could list. We also know that human potential is often stifled—a great and common tragedy. Perhaps one way to say it is that human potential is best expressed through love—whether love of people, one's God, or one's work. Because most people who work in the nonprofit world work there for love, maybe we shouldn't be surprised that many nonprofit groups have become places of realized potential. Maybe we should be surprised only that more organizations haven't bothered to emulate them.

CHAPTER TWO

What's a Movement?

O ver the years, I have become increasingly aware of a singular, qualitative difference among organizations. Most organizations are, well, just organizations, collections of people and assets that serve a purpose. Sometimes they thrive, sometimes they don't. They meet certain needs and have a certain legitimacy in society.

Then there are other, exceptional organizations that we can more precisely call movements. Beth Israel Hospital in Boston (the first hospital in the United States to publish a declaration of patient rights and to incorporate employee and patient ideas into its operations), Willow Creek Church west of Chicago (which reaches out into the unchurched culture rather than expecting all people to reach out to the church), Intervarsity Christian Fellowship in Madison, Wisconsin (a pioneer in Christian ministries in higher education, business, and ethnic cultures), and Apple Computer in its formative years—movements like these dot the organizational landscape and serve as models of energy and devotion to a compelling cause. They illustrate new ways of working together. They set standards of effective function and enlightened contribution. They give us a picture of what a place of realized potential can be.

A movement is a collective state of mind, a public and common understanding that the future can be created, not simply experienced or endured. Many of us never have the good fortune to belong to such a group, where becoming is a way of living and working together.

Movements are easier to recognize from the inside. There is a harmony in relationships and a constructive conflict of ideas. There is a palpable unity as the people there implement their vision. There is a rhythm of innovation and renewal. There's a sense of urgency—movements are never casual. Alongside the normal tensions of organized life, there is a high level of trust.

When I first began to date the girl who later married me, I had to deal with an unexpected phenomenon. I was being introduced into a kissing family. Now it wasn't that I didn't love my own sisters and aunts, but my family just wasn't as demonstrative as Esther's. I had several dates with Esther before I dared ask for a kiss. But Esther's five aunts didn't have any of my timidity; they didn't believe in shaking hands. Each new boyfriend at the family reunion was welcomed immediately with hugs and kisses.

Like kissing families, movements have their distinguishing marks. In movements, people tell stories about giants and about failures. They tell stories about relationships and surprises. They tell stories as a way of teaching. They tell stories as a way of preserving and remembering the past. Movements thrive on their stories.

We are defined by our stories, which continually form us and make us vital and give us hope. Stories teach and preserve traditions and practices and policies and values. I don't know many people who prefer a manual to a myth.

Our fidelity to our stories, like fidelity to choices, shapes our characters and in so doing shapes the movements of which we are a part. Stories play a key role in our movements because they are the vehicles through which we expose and, therefore, greatly reduce the temptation to impose.

Can an organization intentionally shape itself into a movement? It certainly seems reasonable that we can discuss a variety of requirements that movements seem to meet.

One of the first things required in movements is spirit-lifting leadership, leadership that enables, enriches, holds the organization accountable, and in the end lets go.

Also high on the list of requirements is competence. I would expect a movement to be highly participatory, but I would also expect people there to realize that participation and representation are no substitutes for simple competence. Character cannot replace competence. When I think about competence, I mean competence in relationships as well as technical competence, for poor relationships sabotage even the most competent persons. Success in our jobs requires technical competence; success as human beings requires competence in relationships.

A movement requires a high sense of creativity. In some places of realized potential, creativity becomes a moral issue: it is the means through which we protect the human environment. In others it becomes a process of discovery to bring about necessary change. Some of the resulting transitions are actually things the organization can't really afford at the time, but the dangers of equivocation are clear. The transitions will be designed and implemented without fear of either the creative person or the change she brings about.

I remember so well the time in Herman Miller's history when we didn't have money to buy the tool for Charles Eames's first molded fiberglass chair. We all knew that producing the chair was the right thing to do, but how were we going to pay for the tool? Our national sales manager volunteered to loan the company the money—a risky and creative thing for him to do. We bought the tool, and the chair was a great success. Within a short time we managed to repay the money. Thanks to Jim Eppinger, the sales manager, our organization had passed a crucial transition.

One of the beauties of a movement is the clear commitment to substance over bureaucracy. Superficial and trivial activities always give way to a serious concern for content and substance, priorities and discipline. Movements tend to create a wonderful breadth of mind in the people involved, whether the group focuses on human relations or engineering or financial affairs. There arises from the concern for true substance a red thread of optimism and openness about life.

A movement is almost always a civil place, where people respect each other and work for a common good—where they understand that good manners, civil language, and decorum are assets. People respect the constructive mystery of simplicity, fidelity, clarity, and beauty. People are grateful for the contribution of others to their lives and work—even if sometimes we don't quite see how it happens.

When Allan Houser, the great Native American sculptor, was seventy-eight years old, he continued to start each day with a rigorous exercise routine. He knew that if he had no strength in his body, he would not be able to execute the creativity in his heart. One of the wonderful facets of a movement is the existence of disciplined routines in the midst of freedom.

Of course, we have to consider that movements tend to deteriorate into mere organizations.

Some of the signs: we begin to make trade-offs. We begin to prefer comfort to ambiguity. We look for control rather than challenge (it's always easier to deal with commodities than uniqueness). We begin to trust job assignments rather than respecting individual gifts.

I know a young man who has enormous gifts in writing and in music. He's a performer and composer; he's been a filmmaker and writer. He had been plugging away for a number of years in the purchasing department of a large corporation and suddenly found himself, for no reason at all, terminated in a misguided cost-saving cutback. The detour of unemployment soon led him to a new job in a much smaller company doing exactly what his gifts enable him to do best. Not only does he have a bright new life, but his employer has gained an important competitive advantage. His former employers to this day have no idea what they missed—all because they looked too much at assignments and too little at the gifts of persons.

Trouble often comes to movements when we change our common stories—out of embarrassment or because we can't believe or accept them or because the stories suddenly seem naive. New volunteers come with new visions and often without realizing it change history so that the new organization can move like the old. Rewriting history is a risky business. In movements, stories give life; in organizations, stories manipulate people.

Movements suffer when common sense is hailed as innovation, when job descriptions replace expectations, when risky choices become diluted into no-risk decisions, when poets are terminated and bureaucrats promoted, when finishing a project—no matter how routine or unremarkable—is celebrated as an achievement.

Movements ache when leaders lose their sense of dependence on the often quiet but indispensable folks who keep things going so remarkably well day in and day out.

Movements degrade when rules dominate decision making. Some years ago, our family was living in London, where I was working at the time. Both miniskirts and pantsuits were in vogue. My wife had recently purchased a pantsuit with a long jacket. We had guests from the States in our party of seven or eight as we headed for Simpson's in the Strand, whose reputation is still well known, for a good old English dinner of roast beef. The maitre d' took one look at Esther in her new pantsuit, called me off to one side, and informed me that Simpson's did not allow women to wear trousers to dinner. I asked him quietly if Esther would be permitted to wear only her long jacket as a minidress. He immediately agreed to that.

Esther, however, felt differently and had no intention of taking off her trousers. The maitre d' held his ground, and off we went to another restaurant. We have never been back to Simpson's, the restaurant that had for my family, in that moment of truth, become a mere organization.

Finally, and maybe most important, movements suffer when leaders are unable or unwilling to hold the group accountable. Only leaders are able to hold an entire group accountable to itself and to others. If they don't, the movement will become just another organization, having lost its standing in a spirit-quenching moment. When I consider the reasons to work for a movement, it helps to remember this ineluctable fact of life: we are sentenced to live with who we become.

CHAPTER THREE

A Context
for Service

"With liberty and justice for all." I remember those last words from the Pledge of Allegiance, recited dutifully by schoolchildren every day. Now I ask myself a question about those words: liberty to do what? What good is playing tennis (something I used to enjoy attempting every week) without a court?

Like any other virtue, freedom acquires heightened significance when constrained. How do we direct our freedom? To what end do we work? What common good do we serve with all our much defended and much prized freedom? I'm reminded of the second part of a well-known verse from the Bible: "Let my people go, *so that they may serve me.*" As I've already said, many people in the United States give meaning to their freedom by serving others and a common good. Nonprofit organizations have become the chief way for thousands to focus individual efforts into truly marvelous achievements. But what is the context for service in our world today? How can we respond creatively to that context? We don't serve in a vacuum. Neither do we serve without reason.

Is our world more complicated today? Is it more difficult now to serve a common good than it was one hundred or one thousand years ago? Words like *conserve, deserve, preserve,* and *reserve* have certainly been with us for some time. Has *servant* become a pejorative? I'd like to give you some dimensions I've noticed of today's context for service. You will surely have noticed others you can add to this list.

First, we can consider *transition*. For me the idea of transition is one of the most significant ideas that we should be reflecting on today. Transition is a matter and a process of becoming. Transition is a great deal more than change. It's a growing and a maturing and an understanding and wisdom-gaining process. Transition gives us the opportunity to rise above polarization. Transition is a marvelous polishing of our intellectual and spiritual and emotional faculties. It's a process of learning who we are. And it's an opportunity to renew our dreams and refresh our calling. Even if we don't experience transition every day, we must surely prepare ourselves for it.

When I think about a nonprofit group, I don't think of people who hold jobs. I think of folks at

Community Action House in my town who collect and provide food and clothing for others or people who successfully engineer a millage to raise money for parks. These people are responding to a calling, and by its nature a calling requires us to prepare ourselves for any eventuality.

Of course, transitions are risky for organizations, for leaders, for followers. Significant transition is never easy and isn't always aimed at making us more comfortable. Dealing with transition, it seems to me, is only partly a matter of good analysis and problem solving, two activities we've become pretty good at in the United States. It is also a matter of the condition of our hearts. I think we need to bring intuition to transitions in addition to the analytical processes we automatically apply.

I recently came across an old friend who retired about the same time I did. I asked him what he'd been doing, and he said, "I'll be glad to tell you what I'm doing, but I first have to tell you who I am. I'm gifted in two special ways. I'm an excellent organizer and I have gifted hands." You might think with a description like that he's a surgeon. But he's not. Not only is he a professional model maker but he also helps shape the ideas embodied in his craft. He's a woodworker and a contractor. He's using his retirement years to teach other people how to rehab their own homes. What a wonderful example of a person who has gone through the transition of retirement, discovered again who he is, and set a new plan for his life.

Transition is not easy, and it's not assured. There's uncertainty and ambiguity. There are honest differences, there is hostility, and sometimes there are insufficient resources. We see real transition all around us, from our political system, to our schools, to our economic structure. Nonprofits will learn what it takes to become effective in such transition. Yet there are bound to be false steps. I believe the future is going to be uncomfortable, partly because of this definition (sometimes attributed to Einstein but probably apocryphal): "Insanity is when you do the same thing over and over and expect a different result." Yes, there will be insanity, but there will also be eminently sane compassion and good works.

Three books have helped me as I think through transition, and I'd like to recommend them to you. One is Peter Drucker's *Post-Capitalist Society*. Another was written by professor of business Charles Handy, *The Age of Unreason*. The third, written by the mystery novelist P. D. James and completely different from the first two, is *Children of Men*. In various ways these three books discuss the enormous transitions we see all around us, transitions that are shaping our lives and work.

Second, as a great many of us know, *our schools are in the midst of an enormous struggle.* Traditionally our education system has been the focus of countless hours of volunteer work—rightly so, for everything that comes out of the schools comes into society. What comes out of the schools comes into our businesses, our churches, our colleges. What we see in some of our schools right now is not encouraging. In the 1991–92 school year in the Los Angeles school district, teachers and administrators confiscated over fourteen hundred weapons from schoolchildren. Recently one of Esther and my granddaughters, in the 8th grade in the small town of Holland, Michigan, saw two police officers come into her classroom, lead one of her classmates out into the hall, and put handcuffs on him. Are these the marks of a healthy context for education? Our society—which is to say each one of us—will be measured for many years to come by what we are able to do about the education of our children.

Another dimension of the context for service: *the family is at risk.* Is there anybody who doesn't see the risks every day? A powerful, seemingly purposeful denigration of the traditional family is taking place in our society. We suffer from an almost innocent and certainly mindless failure to understand the significance of our loss when we don't aggressively nurture the family and hold it responsible. The traditional family—staying together, holding itself accountable—is the foundation of a civil society. (We'll talk further about the family in Chapter Six.) If we fail our children, the relevance of all other strategies evaporates. Surely we must use our freedom to serve the family—our own families and the larger family of humankind.

Fourth, *our attitude toward assimilation is changing*. The traditional idea of the melting pot of America requires assimilation. But now we have the puzzling problem of dealing civilly and creatively and effectively with significant groups who do not intend to be assimilated or who can't figure out how to be assimilated into American society. In some cases they feel the need to maintain their own language and their own geographical and cultural turf and their own work values. Some are unable to understand or unable to accept the obligations and duties of membership in a free society. Some honestly believe that the practice of victimization is their only road to authenticity.

Our metaphors have changed. We now read about the United States becoming not a melting pot but a salad bowl or mosaic. Whatever the reasons, the reality is that we're in danger of becoming a fragmented nation. A serious threat—and a

real opportunity to serve. However we character-
ize our society, unity at some level remains necessary. If we truly want to serve people, we will
emphasize that one undeniably unifying aspect of
our lives—our language. To have the gift of a single language gives people in the United States a
leg up on our potential. How many of us remember our grandparents saying, "We're too old to
learn English, but you must." For over two hundred years now, a single language has been an
enormous asset to all of us in the United States.
Remember the motto (*not* in English!) on every
coin in your pocket: *e pluribus unum.*

Fifth, *the world of work* is changing in such significant ways and at such a rapid pace that it's one
of the most crucial dimensions of the context in
which nonprofits serve. Three things seem to be
going on simultaneously. Most people on the earth
are trying to get into the agricultural era, some-

thing we in the United States forget. The next largest group of people is trying to move into the industrial era. Finally, the smallest group, those of us in North America, Western Europe, and parts of the Pacific Rim, has moved into the knowledge and information era. Three groups in three different stages of development are at the same time able to see all three eras through the mixed blessing of instantaneous global communication.

It's not surprising that we face enormous tensions in the world of work, with so many people vying for limited resources and the smallest group controlling most of them. Yet what a chance to serve a common good! Surely we can find a way for all societies, whether agricultural, industrial, or information, to progress and serve their members.

Another disturbing development in the world of work is the growing number of permanently part-time workers and even minimally compensated full-time workers who do not make enough money to support a family and who do not receive health care insurance and other benefits. Naturally some people want and need permanent part-time jobs. But many people forced into part-time work cannot maintain the integrity of their families or contribute to the support of their communities—a problem for both individuals and organizations to face up to.

Last in my list of realities with which all of us, but especially nonprofit organizations, must cope is the *growing ambiguity in values*. I see this clearly in the world of work but also in general in our society. The very meanings of words like *truth* and *honesty* and *stealing* and *lie* have grown murky. We see all about us a diminution of personal accountability and moral will. We as a society often acquiesce to simple cheating, lying, and stealing, especially the theft of ideas and creative work. We see all about us examples of a reluctance to put community and a common good ahead of self, a reluctance to make room on the ladder for others.

The concepts of diligence, faithfulness, and trust grow dim, concepts that underlie enormous segments of our economic system. When you stop to think about it, it's astounding that anything as complex as the trading of stocks, bonds, commodities, and futures ultimately depends on trust—a value—not a statute, not an SEC regulation, not even a government mandate. The system works on trust. Yet the fundamental values we have accepted as a society are becoming diluted, thinned to such a degree as to be sometimes unrecognizable. You may deplore this development; you may explain it as the logical result of a pluralistic culture. You cannot deny it. Nonprofit organizations function in light of it.

You may accuse me of constructing not a context for service but an inescapable maze of shifting boundaries and intractable obstacles. We do live in a difficult world and a time of choices. When I was CEO of Herman Miller, I used to have regular meetings with the head of our small security group. Even in the small town of Zeeland, Michigan, we had much of the tragedy and sadness of New York or Chicago, only in a much smaller dose. This man would reveal to me the darker side of things at our company, for Herman Miller, like any organization, is part of the world in which it functions and therefore had the bad with the good. I never avoided hearing the bad news for it raised a simple question about our context. Yes, we all understand that this is the world we live in. We all understand that our world has to change. How shall we change it?

CHAPTER FOUR

What Shall We Measure?

*I*n my experience a failure to make a conscious decision about what it is we're going to measure often causes discombobulation and a lack of effectiveness and a lack of achievement. We're good at talking about what we think about some things, and sometimes we're good at talking about what we believe, and we're often good at talking about what our goals are to be. When it comes time in nonprofit groups to measure, we're not nearly as specific as we ought to be. I think this is true about most organizations. For-profit groups are often adept at measuring many things, but they too often fail to measure the most difficult and the most important achievements and failures.

Now I realize that not everything can be measured, that some matters never end, that failure is always with us. There are mysteries in organizations just as there are mysteries in life. Yet measurement is essential in an organization for several reasons. It's directly connected to the health of the organization. It's directly connected to the way an organization can mature and grow. And it directly affects whether or not we're going to reach our potential—how close we're going to come to our potential. The idea of measurement in an organization is also directly connected to the whole concept of renewal, one of the essential ingredients of which is abandonment. What are we going to give up? What are we going to abandon? None of us has unlimited resources.

The task of stating just exactly what to measure falls to the leaders in organizations. It's not an easy job, and finding what to measure won't happen automatically. Should a college measure alumni involvement? Does Habitat for Humanity measure the number of families finding hope in their own homes? An organization is at sea if it doesn't have a really good idea of what's going to be measured. Once in a cab in Boston I remarked to the driver how much more beautiful and cared for the city seemed to me than it had on my last trip. The cab driver said, "Thank you!" His enthusiastic ownership was a measure of the progress of an entire city.

Let me propose a few things to measure. You'll need your own list, of course, since every organization measures different things. Measurement isn't the complete answer. The best groups measure, learn their lessons, then adjust, then review.

Broadly speaking we can begin by thinking about how we measure inputs and outputs. The Soviet Union believed that in many cases managers should be rewarded with bonuses based on input. If you were running a shoe factory, your bonus as a manager was based on how much leather, how many nails, how many pounds of glue entered the process. If all the shoes came out for left feet, well, that was too bad. Nobody cared—except, of course, the people who needed the shoes. If you made furniture, your bonus was calculated on how many board feet of lumber entered the plant, not on how many chairs came out. A strange system. We should be surprised not that it disintegrated but that it lasted as long as it did.

There are many kinds of inputs to measure. If the Soviets had taken a broader view of inputs, perhaps they would have done better. For instance, what will happen if we think of how a vision is stated and how a vision is translated into a mission as input? How good are we at orienting volunteers to the work we need them to do? How effective are we at giving opportunities for challenge, recognition, and growth to people who serve in nonprofits? I think these are crucial inputs needed from leaders. Dudley Hafner, executive vice president of the American Heart Association, measures input with what he calls "telephone watercooler conferences." Periodically he and his team meet with an invited guest on a forty-five-minute conference call.

Another crucial input: What does the organization expect from people in the way of work? What is it that we expect from each other? Has it been expressed? Nobody's a mind reader.

I remember a time quite a few years ago when our company was having some problems with quality. We're a company that makes systems furniture, and until all the parts of an order had been delivered to the customer, we couldn't very well expect to be paid. Our accounts receivable were always directly related to how much of an order we had shipped, something we had been trying and trying to explain at various corporate meetings. One day when I was out in the plant, a perceptive and articulate lift truck driver stopped me and said, "OK, now let's go through that once more. How is my quality related to those people over there in accounts receivable?" That's a marvelous question. By asking it she did me a great favor because it became an opportunity to lay out expectations.

Clear and relevant planning by project, both for the short term and the long, is an input to be measured—as is our work at appointing the right person to the right job. Especially in nonprofit groups we tend to accept willingness for competence—a dangerous mistake. Willingness is necessary but not sufficient.

Our plans need to be good maps—telling us not where to go but how to make connections. A good annual plan tells everyone in the group how to make connections so that we can move on with our work. Simple discussion together—of the future, of the context in which we serve, of our strengths and resources and weaknesses—can be measured. How well do we discuss who we are and who we intend to be? You know, applying a yardstick to something really can give you a wonderful new insight as to what counts.

Questions and contrary opinions are two more kinds of input. Questions often make us uncomfortable, especially good questions, but they can be the source of insight and the beginning of progress. Often the source of contrary opinions and questions is anonymous. A friend of mine says that he dismisses anonymous letters but that he can't help remembering them. Yet there are good reasons for anonymity, some lying in the setting, some lying in the nature of organizations. After all, we express our opinions anonymously every time we vote. A burden we ought to live with is the need to apply discernment to anonymous letters. Until we're perfect, anonymous letters serve a purpose.

What outputs does an organization need to measure? I think we begin with two things. How does our performance compare to our plan, and how does our performance compare to our potential? It's much easier to extrapolate from the past than to imagine what's possible in the future. Yet the more complex the job, the more important it is to deal with the future. And the more complex the job is, the more talented the people, the higher you want to go on that scale of working on the future.

I don't think, of course, that you can actually measure the future—though I have seen politicians and other prognosticators try. The process of measuring results leads naturally, I think, into the best discussions about the future and about both individual and organizational behavior and potential. How does a seminary measure its results? Not so long ago, it was almost unheard of for a church to fire its pastor. That has changed. Pastors are being fired by the dozens these days, not because they forget their Greek but because some seminaries and some churches are measuring the wrong things and ignoring the future realities of their pastors.

I once posed the following question to a senior vice president of sales and marketing during a performance review: "What would grace enable us to be?" A strange question in a profit-making organization, but I repeated it to the five people for whom I was accountable. The man to whom I first put the question responded with a four-page essay on what grace could enable a corporation in the capitalist system to be. It was an astonishing response. I couldn't measure it, but it gave us such a foundation for a future, such a wonderful forum in which to discuss potential.

It's so easy to fall into the trap of measuring only what's easy to measure. Our real job is to figure out what's significant to the organization and to the people who actually do the work and find ways *together* of measuring what's significant. That's tough. That's essential. That's beginning to reach for potential. Only then can we be faithful to a mission and begin true transition.

It seems to me that we need to accomplish—and accomplishment entails measurement—a few essential things if we in organizations are to do our work. First, understand who we are. Second, define and communicate a vision. Third, accept the vision. Acceptance, not agreement. Organizations could never run if everybody had to agree on everything first. We need confident people who understand what's going on and, whether they agree or not, say, "OK, I'm with you. I'm going to stay on the team. I accept this."

Herman Miller was not organized according to a hierarchical chart. We were organized around about 350 work teams with anywhere from four to twenty-five people on a team. And every work team was related to some other work team. So as the company kept growing, we found ourselves moving from an organization in which some of us knew almost everybody by first name to one of four and five and six thousand people.

This gave us a new problem: How do you maintain a sense of community? How does an organization gain understanding? How do you maintain real communication? My work team and

I decided that the six of us would meet once a month over lunch with volunteers from the company. Everybody would bring lunch, since we didn't want people to feel they were in any way being coerced. We also decided that we had to meet for at least an hour and that the officers could never bring an agenda. Nothing will strangle creative, honest communication faster in a setting like this than an agenda.

After two or three months people found that they could trust these meetings, and they began to raise questions. They asked about this policy or that policy but never asked us to bypass supervisors to make decisions. People didn't ask to champion a personal cause or assuage a pet peeve; they readily understood the bigger picture. Pretty soon we had a waiting list for these lunches, and we found that we were having direct contact with over eight hundred people a year.

We also found that the groups we talked to began to find their own answers—they discovered on their own what they needed to measure. (This mechanism also turned out to be a wonderful continuing education for senior leaders.)

Another way to redefine output is to consider the tone of the body. How is the tone of the body measured in your organization? I think it's a question worthy of an answer.

To measure performance is to gauge a group's sense of urgency. One of the ways in which people try to avoid being measured is by reminding leaders to be more tolerant of the time it takes to get things done. I think actually leaders should be quite intolerant of the time it takes people to get certain things done. (Chapter Nine also discusses this idea.)

One person whom I really admire recently called in somebody who hadn't been performing and said, "I'm going to give you three choices about your job." One, obviously, was to perform better. Another was to volunteer for a different job in the organization for which he might be better suited. The third was to retire early or go to another organization. And the employee said, "Fine, I'll think about that." The supervisor then asked, "How long are you going to think about it?" The reply was, "I was thinking maybe a month." The supervisor said, "I want to know this afternoon." This requirement wasn't cruel; it was taking into account the health of the organization. Time is such an important factor, and we have grown too tolerant of requests for time. Remember that Napoleon told his generals, "Ask me for anything you like, except time."

Is quality in your organization an input or an output? Or is it both? How in your organization would you define quality? I think about quality as a matter of truth. It's an interesting perspective to try, because most of us measure quality only as an attribute of a product we can hold in our hands. Yet quality can be so intangible, and we need some clues as to how we are going to define quality as it pertains to organizational life and work. We can think more about quality in Chapter Seven. To begin to see quality as truth is to begin to define quality for any organization.

How can we measure relationships? Many people in the world of organized work talk about justice today. Justice is high on most people's list of ideas that tell us the way life ought to be. For me, justice in organized life always has to start in terms of relationships. In the for-profit world, the measuring of justice begins in terms of compensation, because it is one of the most real things in each of our lives. Though pay cannot be overlooked in the nonprofit world, justice there begins with the opportunity to make a meaningful

contribution. Remember, we are working primar-
ily for love.

Of course, other measurable aspects affect the
quality of relationships. I think about the level of
trust in the organization. I think about the quality
of communications. I think about the behavior of
leaders, leaders like Frances Hesselbein, who trans-
formed the Girl Scout movement, and John Sawhill,
who is transforming the future of our world
through his work with the Nature Conservancy.

It's interesting how many organizations have
manuals pertaining to technical areas. But for
examples of acceptable behavior we all look naturally and immediately to leaders. Leaders are walking and talking manuals of behavior. As we listen
to them, we silently ask ourselves what they did
last Friday morning when there was a problem.
And we watch. And just as surely as financial people measure return on assets, we all measure

the behavior of our leaders. We measure it against our ideals and against our realities. Think about the return on behavior! Wouldn't that make a telling graph in the annual reports of organizations!

Leaders who realize this know that people expect them to be accountable not so much for control as for equity. We expect leaders to treat everyone the same way. Somebody else can deal with control. Leaders are the guardians of equal access.

Equity is a characteristic of healthy communities, and a healthy community always balances the needs and interests of the group with the needs and interests of persons. While the common good must be held higher than individual gain, everybody has the right to pursue potential. The family and the community and the congregation always come first in building relationships. But what kind of community makes for good soil in which to plant and raise relationships? I think an organization or community or family that's good ground for relationships has what I call, for lack of a better way to put it, good order. It's a place of civility; it's a place of good manners; it's a place of sensitivity; it's a place of forgiveness. All of these aspects have to be in play. They can all be measured.

I recently talked with a man who is a vice president in a large organization. He came to see me and said, "I've got a real problem. My family is breaking up. I've got boys twelve and fourteen years old, and my wife and I are going to get a divorce. I don't know what's going to happen. But I do know that I'm not going to be able to perform up to expectations in my job." And so we talked about it. In the end we decided that he should go to his boss in the same way he had come to me and lay out the circumstances. Be very vulnerable. Run the risk. Somewhat to his surprise, his boss said, "Well, fine. This is a really tough problem, and I'm on your side. I'll start reassigning your work temporarily until you get straightened out. And I want you to know that my wife and I are available to you." Of course, the guy left the meeting in tears. They both did.

Sensitivity and forgiveness can free us all to become more complete individuals and members of communities. It's the right thing to do, but it also pays off.

In building good relationships between leaders and followers, each person has the right to be taken seriously. So long as anybody is part of an organization, he or she is essential. Now it just so happens that leaders more often than followers fall into the trap of failing to take everybody seriously—although I do know some followers who have stopped taking their leaders seriously! But real leaders never forget that every person—

even the naggers, the weak, the overambitious—every person deserves to be taken seriously. Another matter to measure.

These are some thoughts about what to measure if we're to reach toward our potential. In the nonprofit world, qualitative concerns seem so much more appropriate than matters easily quantified. Yet to measure does not always mean to quantify. I can certainly measure my love for my family, though I couldn't quantify it in a million years of trying. I can measure the commitment of the people I see working in the nonprofit world in the lives and happiness of the people they serve, though I find it impossible to quantify that devotion. I can measure the love of teachers for their students in the students' enthusiasm, but the students' test scores hardly indicate their love of learning. I feel certain that the ability of successful nonprofit groups to measure the qualitative issues lies at the heart of their value to society.

As I said in the beginning of this chapter, I realize that not everything can be measured— mystery, beauty, the sweep of a rainbow, the breadth of human potential. Though failure is a reality and sometimes a consequence of mea- surement, continual success probably means our bar is too low or our tape too short.

CHAPTER FIVE

The Language of Potential

A number of years ago on a trip to Russia, long before the collapse of the Soviet Union, I had the privilege of worshiping several times in churches there. Because of the restrictions on the opportunities to worship, the churches were so full that for many there was no place to sit. Stairways were full; aisles were packed. The worshipers had worked out a wonderful system to make the crowding more bearable. During the service people would quietly get up and trade places, the seated with the standing. No one directed this procedure; there was no commotion. What a wonderful expression of community that was. And what a memorable way to communicate!

Leaders are constantly communicating. In fact, I would have to say that leaders communicate more than other people in a group. There is a qualification: most of the time their communication is unconscious and unintentional—like the message of people changing places in the Russian church.

How do leaders communicate? Their language certainly goes beyond mere words. Body language, intuition, presence, accessibility—above all, behavior. We can think about the comparative value of words and behavior. Reality does not inevitably follow words, but we can intimate reality with our language. Followers need to be able to act on the language of a leader; they cannot afford to be mystified or stymied. We need to think about the mind of the beholder, the eye of the beholder. When you're a follower—and we are all followers part of the time—how do you comprehend the language of leaders?

How do you as a leader see yourself? You know, from a follower's perspective, it's vitally important that a leader have a self-perception faithful to reality. I've often noticed the manager of a professional sports team or a member of Congress or a pastor using the phrase "my people." Even though such an expression may rise from the best of motivations and real concern, to the ear of a follower this language reveals a perception 180 degrees from reality. Leaders belong to their followers. A director should refer to employees as "the people I serve." What a different reality that is! And what a different effect on followers.

The first step in learning any language, including the language of potential, is to understand who I am, where I belong, what part I play in this family, church, hospital, or community.

As with all language, substance must come with words. Meaning must be interwoven with expression. We can hardly talk about the language of potential without talking about the beliefs of leaders. Nor should we try to separate the two.

You might say that behavior is the highest form of expression. It also happens to be the most impressive. One day I ran into a person I knew only slightly who said to me, "About ten years ago I was on the same airplane with you flying into Chicago. There was a woman sitting near you with a small child and all that baggage that goes with a small child. I'll never forget that you picked up the child and some of the baggage and carried it into the terminal and helped her find her way through." He ended by saying, "You know, after ten years I've never forgotten that."

Now let me balance that story with one not so flattering. Not long after that, I ran into another person who knows me quite well. He told me about the time he had been sitting a few rows behind me on an airplane when I did not bring my seat back up when I was asked to. I hadn't been listening to the flight attendant. An attendant came along and did it for me. My friend told me that I said to her, "If you do that again, I'll break your arm." He too had never forgotten. Not being mind readers, neither my friend nor the attendant knew that I was protecting a ruptured disk in my back that often responds badly to sudden movements. Even that condition does not excuse my rudeness.

Beyond the advantages of confession, the point of these stories is that long-term consequences always accompany the messages we convey. In this age of ours where crude language assaults us from every direction, we're talking about manners and civility as modes of language. Through our very words, we can demonstrate the virtues of civility and restraint and respect for others.

Let me just give you a few words that I believe are the beginning of the language of potential:

Vision

Healing

Thanks

Forgiveness

Harmony

Please

Momentum

Love

Truth

Service

Unity

Hope

Restoration

The Apostle Paul writes that "you who are spiritual should restore." In the culture of his time, restoring was almost synonymous with the idea of reweaving, of fishermen caring for their nets. Fishermen would weave nets and they would reweave nets, a restoration not only of a tool but of faith in the future.

Restoration, reweaving, is one of the obligations of leadership, an obligation that begins to be fulfilled with the language of potential. When I think about this language therefore, I think about leadership as being both a weaving and a reweaving.

I've often thought that leaders are stumped by serendipity. One day you find yourself being given the gift of leadership as the CEO or the senior pastor or the college president, and a strange thing happens to you. You have become an amateur. Having been given this gift partly because of your expertise in some area or another, you are no longer an expert. There are too many things to know. Having reached the apex of a hierarchy, you're the amateur and totally dependent. You now have to shift from acting as an expert to becoming a quick learner. The organization cannot get from you the decisions you're obliged to make until it teaches you how to make them. That's the only antidote to the Peter Principle.

One of the crucial tasks of leaders—and therefore one of the ends of a leader's language—is to help move groups of people, whether a family or a church or a school, in the direction of maturity as a community. That's when people have the chance to reach their potential. Then you begin to speak the language of potential. Organizations almost never reach their potential without regard to individuals' potential. One way to approach moving toward maturity as a community is to establish what the scientists call critical mass, a sufficient number of people in the community who become advocates for its purpose and mission. It seems to me that there can be a definite process for creating this group of advocates.

First, people in this critical mass need to understand what's going on. Second, they need to accept what the group has agreed to do. Third, they need to behave as advocates.

How would one approach gaining understanding and building acceptance in a specific job setting? I would like to give you a few questions used by an organization actually engaged in the process. Carl Frost, a wise and dear friend, told me about a company in the health care business that raised the following questions in small groups.

Do you know the company's mission? No leader I've ever known can read minds. She has to ask.

Do you understand the supporting data regarding this mission, and do you understand it as a compelling need to change? Many of us go blithely through life thinking we understand the compelling need to change without truly understanding the change required or that the change involves us. You cannot be a participant in a truly worthwhile community unless you understand the compelling need to do something. Do you comprehend the consequences of fulfilling a mission or of failing to do so? That's a neat way of asking, Do you know what the score is and that you could get fired? This is part of understanding the language of potential. Do you comprehend the consequences and are you prepared to live with them?

Do you accept what we as a community are embarked on? The question is not, Do you agree? All of us do many things we don't agree with.

That's pretty natural in our lives, but if we're going to live or work in a true community, then we must connect understanding and acceptance and advocacy. By providing a language, a way of speaking that allows for dissent, disagreement, and expression, we hear the other side, and we reach the best decision.

And of course we must teach ourselves to be vulnerable to people who don't agree with us, to people whose experience forces us to consider a different perception, to welcome our own ignorance. Leaders are comfortable under scrutiny, especially when it comes to their communications, whether verbal or nonverbal. Leaders are comfortable with that scrutiny that adults have a right to, remembering that it's always easier to gossip about poor performance than to confront it.

Are you able and willing to change and to own your share of the problem? If you're going to be a leader who communicates carefully, you may not avoid this kind of a question.

What are you going to bring in terms of competence, contributions, and commitment to this project? I would gladly follow a leader who asks that kind of question. If I'm going to be an authentic member of a team, I'd like to know what's expected of me, and I'd really like to have a leader ask me what I'm bringing to the game.

In this arena we have to put a special emphasis on trust, which can never occur without truth. We must be able to trust leaders to listen, to listen well, and to see. We must be able to trust them to be able to see pain. Leaders need to be able to see heartbreak. Leaders need to be able to see achievement. A leader needs to work very hard at developing the ability to see what's really going on in an organization.

I have a friend who graduated from General Motors Technical Institute and came to work at Herman Miller. He proposed that we get together every three months for lunch. And so our relationship grew into what people now refer to as a mentor relationship. Once he asked me if I knew anything about business schools. He was wondering whether he should get an M.B.A. I don't know much about the subject, but we talked about it for a little while. I said to him, "There's one thing I'd like to know before I at least offer any suggestions about your getting an M.B.A. Ordinarily one sees graduate education as a response to a felt need. What in your life are you the least good at?" "Oh," he said, "that's easy. You know I've got a wife and I've got these two little boys, one is five and one is three, and I don't know anything about being either a husband or a father." I said, "Well why are you worried about an M.B.A.?"

This conversation could only have happened with trust. Trust is the required subtext behind almost everything leaders say if the language of potential is to have any real meaning or effect. How many times do we see leaders who speak in front of large groups but they themselves are the only people listening? Without trust a leader's language might as well be Greek.

Much of the language of potential has to do with the language of teaching and learning. Leaders or followers, we're all faced with a mandate to become lifetime learners. We simply won't survive in an information and knowledge era unless we become lifetime learners. Charles Handy in his wonderful book *The Age of Unreason* says that within fifteen years 80 percent of the people in the Western world (he includes the Pacific Rim) are going to be making their living with cerebral skills, not manual skills. We'll all be living by our wits.

I would like to suggest that there are three areas in which we need to think about the language of teaching and learning. First, whether you work for a book publishing company, whether you work for a major hospital, whether you work in a homeless shelter, there's a technical side to your work.

Next, we have to become competent in relationships. Almost no one is going to have the luxury of working alone. All of us are going to be working in ways in which we're interdependent with other people. And the only way we can do that effectively is to build competence in relationships.

Third, we need to become much more skilled in affecting the context in which we're going to be working. Perhaps that's why I have such admiration for movements like the Salvation Army and Food Gatherers. They are working to change our context for the better. Are we going to create for ourselves and our organizations a context where learning and teaching are as common as hierarchy, lunch breaks, and financial reckonings?

This brings me to the language of touch, a part of the language of potential about which we want to think metaphysically and physically. We have to understand what kind of animal we humans are. And we have to understand what our needs are. We have to begin to learn again how—in these times of legislated restraint—to speak to each other in the language of touch. There are times when a public hug or a public kiss is exactly what an organization needs. I don't think we can prescribe any rules for that, but I do think we have to begin to think more carefully about renewing the ministry or the language of touch in our communities.

Years ago I had a mentor tell me that it's okay to put your arm around the shoulder of a person only if you're not going to take something away.

Another way to think about touch is to remember that only through touch are plans and agendas and visions made real. Only through action can a language—any language—ramify itself in our world. For that, leaders and followers are necessary. For that, communities are required.

CHAPTER SIX

Service Has Its Roots

*M*ajor college coaches recruit carefully and diligently because they know their success as coaches depends on their recruits' potential. They know the high school coaches who turn out the best-prepared players. Coaches reach their own potential by combining the natural gifts of the young people they recruit and the context in which those gifts have been shaped.

Like successful coaches (and I do believe that not all successful coaches win), every effective organization has a high regard for the sources of its recruits. This applies equally in the for-profit and not-for-profit worlds. It's apparent that the family is the soil in which competence, productive relationships, and a commitment to service take root. The family is where learning and love and life begin. The family is where accountability begins, because healthy families hold themselves accountable. If you've read my other books, you'll know by now that I'm not normally given to making pronouncements. But I feel so strongly about the importance of families that I feel I must say that families are in real trouble. Most people already know that.

Families are still the first place where most of us learn that we don't always have to get our own way. Families are still where most of us first learn the simple distinctions of life. Colin Powell, during the 1996 Republican Party Convention, said about his parents, "Integrity, kindness, and godliness, they taught us, were right. Lying, violence, intolerance, crime, drugs were wrong, and even worse than wrong, in my family, they were shameful." How necessary distinctions like these are before we can even begin to think about potential! A young pastor friend of mine was once trying to teach gang members about forgiveness. They were having trouble understanding, when one bright boy asked my friend about right and wrong. "You have to know the difference between right and wrong," the boy said, "before you can learn about forgiveness."

We also learn to judge competence in families. Whether you are in charge of employee orientation at McDonald's or you work for NASA, there is a technical side to your business. Whether you work at World Vision helping people throughout the world learn how to survive or at Meredith Publishing in Des Moines, there is a specific technical competence required. The ability to become proficient at any technical aspect of work begins at home, for there we see—or we don't see—some kind of competence demonstrated. In our families we witness—or we don't—the expression of interdependency. In our families we learn—or we fail to learn—what it means to commit ourselves to a common good.

It doesn't surprise me to realize that nonprofit groups are both especially dependent on families and peculiarly suited to help them. In fact families can be the prototypical place of realized potential, and the attributes of vital organizations (the ideas we'll discuss in Chapter Seven) apply to families as well as to other groups. When we stop to think about it, a healthy family is perhaps the best example of a nonprofit group!

Several years ago I served on the Board of Michigan Future, Inc., a lively, diverse group of people seriously contending to improve Michigan's economic competitiveness, its education system, and its families and neighborhoods. A list of tasks for families resulted from our work together. I think you'll see the interesting parallels between families and nonprofit organizations as you read through this list. Add your own items in the margins.

Families must provide unconditional love. Somebody has to be crazy about you. Many nonprofit groups I know make it their business to be crazy about the people they serve. It's the basis for their success and their service. Families love us because of who we are, not because of what we do or don't do.

Families must teach and demonstrate a clear, concrete set of values. Every group needs a set of values by which to operate. Nonprofits and families especially need to be clear about what they believe, and they need to act out those beliefs. I mean a way of looking at life and relationships, relationships to other people, to the community, and even to our country. Who would ever give her spirit to a nonprofit with beliefs that didn't gibe with her own?

In a family at least one person must work. We learn about the importance of work only in our families. Work and its ramifications cannot be grasped theoretically. We have to see it in action. Organizations—including the best nonprofit groups—are not ordained to survive and prosper. Neither are even the happiest of families. Survival in all cases is a function of belief and action. The importance of work is enormous.

Families must teach appropriate social and functional skills. Life in families, like life in organizations, requires us to understand and appreciate and work with other people. Human relationships are not an abstraction of sociologists. They are required in organized life, and we learn to form them in our families.

Neither are functional skills an abstraction. Families are where we learn to buy a car, or arrange for a mortgage, or pay the rent—things you don't learn in school. Families teach us manners and respect—both respect for others and respect for ourselves. Above all, families teach us the importance of expectations.

Families must teach us how to manage resources. No one and no organization functions with limitless resources. Experience and education teach us many things about managing resources, but our ability to see the necessity for managing what we have begins in our families.

Families must teach us how to see learning as a permanent part of life. We all know that organizations must learn and grow to survive, and organizations learn and grow only when people learn and grow—this is the foundation for hope. We must know how to ensure learning, a process that begins in families. Learning and hope are inextricably woven together—both depend on, and result from, our capacity to conceive a future for ourselves and the people we love.

Families must explore the future together. Volunteer work, as many people have discovered, usually becomes a path to growth. But where do we learn to share a common future? In our families we learn how to build a concept of the future. We learn to plan. We discover the beauty of deferred gratification. We learn about the contributions that others make to our lives. We explore options and experiment with choices. This is what a future is all about.

Families celebrate together. We celebrate not only achievement but simple joy in improving our family and the lives of people in it. Celebration is a form of nurture. We don't often enough set out to celebrate, even though we know that celebrations become milestones marking performance and maturity and achievement. Celebrations have real substance in our lives.

One of the most serious needs in organizations is to prepare continually for the future. I'd like to suggest that what we do about reestablishing the family is the most significant action we can take to prepare for the future.

I believe nonprofit organizations have the commitment and the heart and the competence to lead this effort. We have rich inventories of talent and resources to share. We can establish and nurture strong two-way mentoring programs in our organizations and communities. I am convinced that nonprofits, in reaching for their potential, have both a golden opportunity and a unique responsibility in these arenas. In short, if nonprofits are to enjoy the tree of a commitment to service, they must tend to the roots.

One year my oldest daughter decided she was ready to buy a car. It's an experience most of us have sooner or later. She asked me to go along. As we were talking, Jody told me she thought she wanted to buy a Porsche. Trying hard to hide my astonishment at her choice, I asked her if she had checked out the prices and the cost of insurance. Not yet, she told me, and on we went toward the Porsche dealer. Jody's eyes opened wider and wider as she looked at the price tags on the cars. Later, we checked into the cost of insurance, and Jody's eyes opened even wider. (As I recall, the insurance on a Porsche equaled one-third of Jody's annual earnings!) After some sobering discussion about her finances, she decided to buy a small Volkswagen. Of such small experiences is family life filled, made possible by concern and true love. Upon such experiences are constructive lives in organizations and service to a higher good built every day.

CHAPTER SEVEN

Attributes of Vital Organizations

*H*ow do we know a vital organization when we see one? I'm not sure how, but we do. What qualities give an organization vitality? Vital organizations exude health and energy and enthusiasm. Like vital people, they are full of hope and anticipation for things to come. Confident of their own place in time and space, they respect their history without being ruled by it. They look at their own PR and only half believe it.

Over the years I have observed many attributes of vital organizations, examples of which I see all the time in the nonprofit world. These attributes enable and enrich life in those organizations. They enhance achievement. They focus on faithfulness before success. They move the organization always toward potential as opposed to goals. They allow people to realize their own potential.

With those ideas in mind, I'd like to propose a list of organizational attributes that seem to appear regularly in organizations we admire. I hope that you will add your thoughts.

TRUTH

What is the nature of truth? The New Testament says—and I believe—that truth is a person. I think truth is also quality. The poet John Keats would have us believe that truth is beauty, and in many cases it is. Truth can at times be a promise. Truth can be a communication. There are many wonderful ways in which to think about the concept of truth.

Eberhard Jungel, an East German theologian and philosopher, wrote a perceptive essay after the fall of the Berlin Wall. In it he said, "If one begins to analyze why realized socialism [the insider's term for totalitarianism] finally failed, one should seek the decisive cause in its objective untruthfulness." We're familiar with the objective untruthfulness of government, of corporate advertising, of dysfunctional families. We are almost adjusted to it. The great sadness of denying truth is that we all become accomplices in our own spiritual demise.

At the company I worked for, kiosks and bulletin boards were a part of the communication system. People put their own advertisements up, their own versions of truth. I will never forget the one that said, "For sale, wedding dress, worn once, by mistake." This is the opposite of objective untruthfulness.

Sojourner Truth was one of the best-known "conductors" on the Underground Railroad before and during the U.S. Civil War. Her beautiful name expresses for me the elusive and hopeful and luminous nature of truth. It seems to me that in our most private moments, we all know truth in our hearts.

ACCESS

Like talent and wealth, access is a gift. It needs to be shared because it demands accountability. Access to opportunity; access to medical care; access to work, a mentor, a leader, a chance to learn; access to fruitful and healthy relationships— access is a marvelous thing, but there's a growing dearth of it in our society. In vital organizations there is no dearth of access.

We have a growing number of people who don't have access to good medical care or to a good education or to a place to live or to the opportunity of work. And so we have to understand that access is one of the values of a good organization.

Some time ago at Herman Miller a father called in and told his supervisor, "My son was picked up last night for drunk driving, and I don't know how to get him out of jail." The supervisor needed the father back at work, and the family needed help. We discovered that to be a well-rounded supervisor you had to learn how to raise bail. That's a part of access.

DISCIPLINE

I put discipline in the same category with delegation, crucial elements that leaders owe to individuals. You're not being fair to somebody if you don't delegate some of the important work. And you're not being fair to a person if you don't require discipline in terms of the organization's needs. We are prone to create problems by putting people in the wrong jobs without considering and without telling them what the group needs. We don't recognize their gifts. We assign work that needs to be done, but we don't bother to connect the work to the gifts of people.

Discipline applies to many other parts of work in organizations, and I always remind myself that discipline among followers mirrors the discipline demonstrated by leaders.

ACCOUNTABILITY

We need accountability—organizational and personal, to and for others—not blame. Nonprofit groups make themselves accountable to the people they serve, an obligation far beyond a corporation's commitment to its customers. Many nonprofit groups labor long and hard with very little thanks or recognition, sustained only by their own conviction that what they are doing is the right thing.

NOURISHMENT FOR PERSONS

People are nourished by transforming work, growth, reaching their potential. I believe very strongly that only by continually renewing its members can an organization continually renew itself. A vital organization is full of vital individuals. The organization can never be something that I as a member don't choose to be.

Vital organizations have adopted an attitude of lifetime learning, and they help their members make everyday learning a reality in their lives. The nourishment of individuals lies at the heart of vitality in organizations, and the nourishment of individuals begins with the opportunity to learn.

AUTHENTICITY

We are created, I believe, in the image of God, a belief surrounded by enormous moral and ethical implications. Vital organizations don't grant their members authenticity; they acknowledge that people come already wrapped in authentic humanness. When an organization truly acknowledges the a priori authenticity of each person and acts accordingly, how many ways open up for people to reach their potential!

JUSTICE

The heart of justice in organizations is relationships constructed on right practice. When it comes to compensation, that most practical part of life in organizations, how do you think in terms remotely connected to justice?

Some time ago the board of Herman Miller went through a search for a new CEO. We had some marvelous candidates, and we asked each of the eight finalists, "Can you live with the policy of a cap on your salary? Can you live with a salary in a specified relationship to the salaries of everyone else in the company?" In every case the answer was yes, both from the point of view of a personal philosophy and from the practical point of view of being competitive in the marketplace. Justice is always related to everybody in the organization.

Any discussion of justice also brings to mind Martin Luther King's wonderful distinction about peace. There is, he said in his "Letter from a Birmingham Jail," the "negative peace which is the absence of tension," and the "positive peace which is the presence of justice."

RESPECT

In our organizations respect for each other is shown in civility, in good manners, and in language, each of which is an expression of the heart and mind. Respect becomes palpable when everyone is taken seriously, and respect in vital organizations becomes manifest in action. Simple good manners are evidence of respect. Such a deep thinker as Peter Drucker said long ago that manners are the lubricant of an organization.

HOPE

The creating of hope is such an important function of vital organizations that I have spent a whole chapter (Chapter Eleven) discussing it. I'll say here that in healthy families and vital organizations people find hope everywhere they look. Vital organizations also generate hope.

WORKABLE UNITY

John Gardner advises us in his wonderful book *On Leadership* to build a workable level of unity.

In my view, Gardner's idea implies that we have to learn how to transform organizations into communities. It is not only the right thing to do, it's the very best thing to do. A community performs on a much higher level than an organization.

A workable unity is a lavish bringing together, and technology is no substitute for relationships— computers and local area networks do not smile or say hello. They are not aware of a stifled groan and do not notice a moist eye.

TOLERANCE

Tolerance is a function of wisdom, discernment, acceptance not agreement, promise keeping, inclusiveness. Of course simple tolerance is only the beginning of a community, but tolerance is rare enough these days. If we work together toward a common good, I should not insist that you think like me or live as I do. Your commitment to a common vision and agreed-on goals is sufficient to establish a working relationship.

SIMPLICITY

Vital organizations, like vital individuals, understand the role of personal restraint in life. America has become a materialistic society and a powerful society. Just because we can make a weapon doesn't mean we should. Just because we can afford something doesn't mean we should have it. Vital organizations respect and practice conservation and simplicity. Why are some people, with everything money can buy and nothing money can't, surprised that what really counts is still missing? Vital organizations are rich in the acquisitions of the spirit.

Restraint and conservation are also essential to renewal and innovation—to take hold of one thing you have to let go of something else. Unless you happen to have more than two hands.

BEAUTY AND TASTE

Václav Havel, who served far too short a term as the president of Czechoslovakia and is now president of the Czech Republic, wrote many things even while in the middle of an enormous transition both in his nation and his personal life. Much of what he has written, whether he intended it or not, applies directly to us in the United States. When he moved into the president's office in Prague, he was immediately struck by the obvious and simple ugliness of it all, the poor taste in art and decoration. It wasn't difficult, he said, to understand why communism was such a poor form of government.

FIDELITY TO A MISSION

We show fidelity to a mission through strict observance of our promises. Fidelity to a mission is the realization of commitment. Words made flesh.

Now to me there's a nuance in thinking about truth at the beginning and fidelity at the end. To me fidelity is a sincere keeping of one's promises. That's crucial in the life of the follower. If you think about all of these things, they emanate from what's important to a follower. The best nonprofit groups begin with truth and end with fidelity to their missions.

Vital organizations have the innocent energy of children and the compassionate wisdom of older people. They exist all around us, especially in the world of not-for-profit work. Perhaps organizations become vital because the people in those groups bring vitality with them. Or perhaps the organization elicits vital contributions from the people who work there. I suspect it is a little of both.

When I think of vital organizations, I think of the Apostle Paul's request of the Philippians: "Whatever is true, whatever is honorable, whatever is just, whatever is pure, whatever is lovely, whatever is gracious, if there is any excellence, if there is anything worthy of praise, think about these things." Vital organizations do more than think about these things. They epitomize them.

CHAPTER EIGHT

Vision

A child making a sand castle

has some kind of picture in his head

telling him what to do next.

—GEORGE NELSON, *HOW TO SEE*

*F*or years George Nelson, that delightful combination of industrial designer, author, and design thinker, worked with Herman Miller. On many occasions I was lucky enough to work with George and watch him puzzle out a design or a sentence.

In his instructive and entertaining book about design, *How to See,* George discusses the ins and outs of how and why we perceive things the way we do. In the beginning of his book George observes, in that matter-of-fact way of his, that "we all tend to see in terms of what we know and believe." His observation makes me consider the distinction between sight and vision and the importance of both to organizations. People without sight develop other abilities; people without vision constantly struggle to find hope. Organizations without a view of reality may stumble along for a while but will never succeed. Organizations without vision remain mere organizations, surviving but not living, hitting temporary targets but not moving toward potential.

Perhaps a way to think about the difference between sight and vision is this: we can teach ourselves to see things the way they are. Only with vision can we begin to see things the way they can be.

Part of an organization's vision can be an ideal toward which we always strive without ever reaching it. Part of a vision must be attainable, lest the group lose hope. A good idea does not a vision make. Without some risk attached, a good idea remains nothing more. With some risk, with some promise of change, with a touch of the unattainable, a good idea may just become the vision for a group. Visions are liable to fail. A vision can never be guaranteed, no matter what the price or source.

A group's vision can come from one person or many people, but leaders constantly explain and elucidate it. Good visions become clouded when leaders can't separate themselves from the issues or become afraid of the consequences the vision demands. Sometimes nothing can fulfill a vision. When a leader or a group lacks resources or competence, nothing will save even their grandest vision of the ways things might be. Sometimes an organization's structure cannot contain a vision, and it is left to people outside the organization to make the vision reality.

A vision often becomes a question for a group. Can we become what we are not now? Experience teaches us that the quality and usefulness of our answers depend on the appropriateness and insight of our questions. Here is my list of questions about vision. I hope my list will spark more questions from you.

Why must we have vision?

What can vision do for us?

Why is vision valuable?

Does our vision give us hope? Or is it simply a fantasy?

How do we make use of vision?

Can we connect our vision to our daily tasks?

Who gets it? Why some but not others?

How is vision related to renewal or
innovation?

Is vision a part of our "creative force"?

Is vision analogous to beauty?

Against what can vision become a barrier?

Is vision our bottom line?

What kind of vision gives an organization
health?

How does vision relate to our potential?

What can vision teach us about ourselves and
our organizations?

How can a vision unite, inspire, and give
purpose?

Our society is full of nonprofit groups inspired
by visions of the world as it might be. Their visions
give the rest of us hope, but we cannot see the

vision until it becomes real. And perhaps that becomes another distinction between sight and vision: insiders have a vision; outsiders can at best see only the results.

CHAPTER NINE

Trust Me

W hile I was working in Europe in the late 1960s, our family vacationed for a week in Marrakech, Morocco. In addition to touring the High Atlas Mountains and sampling new and exotic food, we did our share of shopping in the souks, the local markets full of life and color and sound. We specifically looked for one of the wonderful, colorful handmade wool rugs we had seen everywhere there, and we had fun looking at dozens of rugs, focusing on a few, finally selecting one. Then began the separate process of bargaining over the price. The transaction involved

English and French, two or three required exits from the shop, and the inevitable return with a counteroffer. At last we had a deal.

Then we faced a problem. The rug was to be shipped to our home in Michigan, but we would be living in Basel and London for another six or eight months. The shop owner, of course, wanted a check or a credit card immediately. Sensing our uncertainty about what to do, he told us that naturally we would need some way to verify back in Michigan that we had the rug we were buying. He proposed that I sign my name in dark blue indelible ink on the underside of the rug. After twenty-five years and several cleanings, my signature shows clearly on our rug, the symbol of a mutual and spontaneous trust between American tourists and a Moroccan merchant.

In organized life, leaders covet trust. Many like to say they would give their right arms for it. They are often frustrated by the mystery surrounding trust and its origins. So little trust seems to be alive in organizations, and it disappears even as we think we have firmly established it.

Followers too yearn for trust. They want badly to believe their leaders and to trust them to do what they say they will do. To be effective and productive, followers must be able to trust and be trusted. Followers seem to have a more reliable intuition about trust and its healthy effects than many leaders give them credit for. When trust permeates a group, great things are possible, not the least of which is a true opportunity to reach our potential.

Trust has its roots. Trust has its stories. Trust is often most eloquently expressed in secrets. Trust has its signals. Driving through Ireland I frequently came across a simple sign—Community Alert—announcing that the residents were committed to watching out for one another. This was a sign of community trust. These people had entrusted their houses and children and community to one another. My friend Lew Smedes writes in his most recent book, "Only trust holds personal relationships—friendship, marriage, family, or a larger community—together."

Trust in organizations is functional. Communications, relationships, unity—so much depends on trust. When things go awry, trust powers the generators until the problem is fixed.

Trust has its values. The beginnings of trust lie in our families, our schools, our models and mentors, our churches, our clubs and teams. Imagine how many people would be disappointed if we required an umpire or referee for every game!

Yet for all the trust that exists in our world, it is not an inevitable result of organizing ourselves into groups. Even in nonprofit organizations, where we might expect it to blossom more readily, trust must be cultivated. Leaders quickly learn that followers set standards to be met before trust is granted. Perhaps that's a reason trust is so precious in organizations: it cannot be bought or commanded, inherited or enforced. To maintain it, leaders must continually earn it. A position of trust is not a lifetime sinecure.

Trust does not arrive in our portfolio of skills when we accept a new job, profess good intentions, or adopt a new "management style" (whatever that strange phrase means). Trust springs from a serious pursuit by both leaders and followers of at least seven essential beliefs and initiatives.

Trust begins with a personal commitment to respect others, to take everyone seriously. Respect demands that we first recognize each other's gifts and strengths and interests; then we must integrate them into the work of the organization. Only then can we reach our common and individual potentials. To take people seriously requires us to listen seriously.

The West Michigan Whitecaps baseball team draws capacity crowds nearly every night of the summer in Grand Rapids, Michigan. At a game in the summer of 1995, one of the Whitecaps' players hit a sharp ground ball to the opposing shortstop, who was unable to get the ball out of his glove, and the runner was safe at first. The shortstop, apparently feeling morose about his error, began to walk slowly toward the mound to hand the pitcher the ball when the runner took off for second. The second baseman hadn't bothered to go over to cover the bag, and the runner was easily safe. After a few minutes the official scorer, not knowing exactly how to score such a play, announced over the public address system that he had decided simply to write off the second error to "defensive indifference." How many errors in organizations are due to leadership indifference?

To tell capable people how to do their job, even innocently or with the best intentions, crodcs trust. Such "advice" becomes a sign of disrespect for followers. How can I trust you if you believe you are better at my job than I am?

Trust grows when people see leaders translate their personal integrity into organizational fidelity. At the heart of fidelity lies truth telling and promise keeping. In organizations truth is not, as some like to think, power. Truth sets us frcc. Truth gathers no adjectives. We know that truth's nakedness leads us either toward trust or away from it. Truth is the gift of liberty and clears the ground for trust. Without truth, trust becomes overshadowed and stunted by the undergrowth of partial lies and outright falsehoods.

The moral purpose of our organizations and of our personal commitments is the soil in which trust can take root and grow. Many years ago Peter Drucker reminded me in talking about leadership that "the eye of the farmer is the best manure." Our character and experience and beliefs allow trust to mature. Like values, moral purpose needs to be an open book in organizations seeking their potential. It needs to be expressed and debated and repeated.

In her wonderful book *Death and Life of Great American Cities,* Jane Jacobs describes safety on the streets as the consequence of people in the apartments above keeping an eye on things below—a shared responsibility of taking care of other people that gives moral purpose to our lives. Moral purpose understood, accepted, and practiced as a common conscience is a special treasure of nonprofit society. It dearly needs to be emulated in other sectors of American life. (We can think more about moral purpose in Chapter Thirteen.)

Trust is built on kept promises. Leaders who keep their promises and followers who respond in kind create an opportunity to generate enormous energy around their commitment to serve others. Conversely, promises made insincerely or promiscuously—promises used to manipulate or to posture—quickly become apparent to followers, clients, or one's constituencies. Few things chip away at trust as effectively as broken promises.

I like to remember that to be chosen means to be *entrusted.*

Trust in organizations depends on the reasonable assumption by followers that leaders can be depended on to do the right thing. My friend Paul Nelson, president of Aquinas College in Grand Rapids, likes to tell students (and I suspect faculty members as well) that good character is expressed in "the making of the nobler choice." And what else is volunteer service all about?

In some areas of our work—the creative or innovative parts, for example—leaders should not always be predictable. In most cases though, from the perspective of followers, it is essential that leaders predictably, dependably, and consistently do the right thing. Predictability in organizational leaders is a virtue that contributes to trust and allows followers the freedom to move toward goals and potential on their own.

What is the right thing? Since every organization is different, finding the right thing is a difficult, varying, and elusive determination to make for all of us. Perhaps we can think of it as the instinct of true leaders in all parts of the organization.

The building of trust in organizations requires leaders to hold the group accountable. This obligation has a special connection to trust and has gone without much attention. Organizations must teach themselves what to measure and then periodically evaluate their performance. While some of this may be done among peers, in the end only the leader can hold the entire group—as a group—accountable. As a matter of experience the group looks to the leader to do this. When a leader is unable or unwilling—when she is not intimate enough with what the group intends to be or how it is progressing toward its potential— to hold the organization accountable, she is guilty of a major betrayal of trust. I know of few things in otherwise fine organizations that will so quickly wither the spirit as the leader's failure to hold the organization accountable. (I might add that by holding accountable I do not mean blame. True accountability belongs to everyone. Blame does not belong in places of realized potential.)

For trust to be maintained over time, leaders must demonstrate competence in their jobs—just like everyone else. The effectiveness of a leader reads like an open book to followers and peers. Leaders have few secrets when it comes to competent performance under the scrutiny of followers. An outside board can't compare to insiders when it comes to evaluating the performance of a leader. In genuine movements, where we are reaching for potential in addition to success, leaders demonstrate competence day in and day out. An important challenge.

Leaders will explain to the organization (that is, make a promise) how they intend to do their jobs on behalf of the group, how they will build on the group's strengths, how they will make difficult choices. They will describe how the leader and the group will achieve a mission together and what the organization should measure. By doing these tasks well, leaders clear a path for followers, show them how they will fit into the picture and how they can do their jobs in sync with others. This process becomes one of the important teaching duties of leadership.

Achieving significant results, in both the for-profit and the nonprofit worlds, springs from long-term focus and commitment and discipline. Implementing a strategy, preparing an organization for change, hewing to a mission—all of these require action over time. All of these require, and result in, trust.

One of the quirks of the American perspective, especially the American corporate perspective, is the tendency to equate speed and time. At many levels in an organization, time management is important. When leaders must deal with the fundamental issue of corporate survival, however, time management often masks the failure to establish priorities or create the discipline to stick to them. My dictionary says of speed, "quickness, promptness, or dispatch in the performance of some action or operation." It says about time, "the length of time sufficient, necessary, or desired for some purpose." Two very different ideas.

You don't reach your potential in the same way you get a job done.

Building trust in organizations has become a chief responsibility of leaders, an essential duty especially in the eyes of followers. True leaders take time (rather than insisting on speed) to develop the persistence, the patience, and the discipline that will ultimately result in trust. As a mark of trust, leaders lean hard on followers and vice versa. Do we ever truly count on people we don't trust?

I grew up in a family of seven children during the Great Depression, that chaotic and perilous and wonderful time when acts of trust occurred every day in front of the common sign "In God we trust. All others pay cash." Of course not very many people had cash to begin with; trust had to do. Everybody in my family chipped in—making beds, hanging the wash outdoors in winter, stoking the coal furnace before school, canning meat and vegetables. It may have irritated us kids, but it never hurt us. Our mother, a born leader, always assigned work with the same admonition: "Don't just give it a lick and a promise." We knew what she meant. We knew that if something wasn't done well the first time, we'd soon do it again.

My mother's marching order applies to leaders trying to build trust. Earning trust is not easy, nor is it cheap, nor does it happen quickly. Earning trust is hard and demanding work. Trust comes only with genuine effort, never with a lick and a promise. My mother would also have told you that it's much more difficult to rebuild trust than to build it in the first place. Once we have built it, we should treasure and protect it. Trust can be won only slowly; it can be lost in the twinkling of an eye.

CHAPTER TEN

Why Risk It?

We all know people who like to be near the water but not in it. They would rather sail without wind. When our kids were teenagers, we lived on Lake Michigan and had a twelve-foot catamaran. On a really good windy day you can almost pull a water-skier on Lake Michigan with a twelve-foot catamaran. But you can't do that, and you can't learn how to sail, without wind. You can't learn how to sail a boat until you've tipped it over a few times. Sometimes we think we're a little too gifted to show up, you know. But none of us truly is. This, to me, describes the central conundrum of risk. By avoiding risk we really risk what's most important in life—reaching toward growth, our potential, and a true contribution to a common good.

The vocabulary of risk reveals a great deal about how we feel about it. We use a variety of phrases in connection with risk—minimizing the risk, spreading the risk, reducing the risk, running the risk, risk-prone, risk-averse, balancing the risks, risky business, worth the risk.

Is taking risks any easier in the volunteer sector than in the for-profit sector? Is there a difference between a risk for love and a risk for gain? For instance, no matter what one thinks personally about the politics of the American Civil Liberties Union, one has to admire their consistent risk-taking—risk seems to be inherent in who they are. To join any organization requires us to risk something—our egos, our commitment, our energy. Yet to join an organization purely to serve is a special kind of risk. Wherever or however we serve, we can't avoid the central conundrum of risk: to risk nothing is perhaps the greatest risk of all.

It's interesting to reflect on what it is we risk. Sometimes we risk the present, and we do so most often consciously. Most of the time we risk the future, and we usually do so unconsciously. Many times we think about risking only material things. But in subtle, unspoken collaboration, we often risk persons and their future and their potential. In fact the degree to which we are prepared to take risks determines the degree to which we as individuals and as organizations can reach our potential.

Organizations often unwittingly risk their very characters in the heat of temporary fires that threaten, we think, to consume everything. Often these fires turn out to be mostly smoke, and we discover too late that the risks lay not where we supposed but in an entirely different quarter.

Risk is often defined for us by circumstances. The cartoon character who risks murder and mayhem isn't really risking anything at all. Road Runner's old adversary Coyote always returns from blasting or squashing as good as new in a few seconds. But in reality, in the hills of Bosnia or the ruined neighborhoods of Detroit or Los Angeles or the South Bronx, hurts don't disappear, not for the people who live there or for the many volunteers who move there to help. The Peace Corps volunteers who live in Africa to teach people to farm or to read take real, physical risks, and some pay the price.

Risk is not only defined for us by circumstances but also frequently resides in our relationships. Risk can be like an open book. It can also be mysterious. Risk undoubtedly has a relationship to change. In very real change, at least, risk seems to be the essential ingredient. I'm convinced from many years of experience that the success of both innovation and renewal in organizations depends on the degree of risk the group is prepared to take. Perhaps that is another way of saying, "nothing ventured, nothing gained."

Through experience and through trial and error and through evaluating results, we choose people to whom we will delegate important responsibilities. We select engineers and researchers and designers and agree on what projects we should tackle together. The best results, the truly beneficial surprises, come from selecting the right person and giving that person the freedom to do what we cannot ourselves do. In my experience in working with creative people, the writer or the designer or the architect is in the end most qualified to decide the result. Yet many people in the corporate world consider it a risk of the highest order to give specially talented people this kind of responsibility. An even greater risk, it seems

to me, is to assign important work to incompe-
tence and, a related risk, to mistake presence and
enthusiasm for true experience and competence.
The nonprofit world often delegates important
work to people without the right experience simply because most volunteers come brimming over
with enthusiasm.

We hear and read much about risks for gain.
Pundits warn us of the risks in the stock market
and preach about the necessity of taking risks in
corporations. Of course all the talk doesn't make
it any easier for people in the for-profit world to
take risks. There is an inherent paradox at work
here: we risk what exists to add to the pile, and a
larger pile makes it more difficult to take a risk
the next time. Still, people and corporations do
find the courage to take risks for the right reasons.
A friend of mine, Lyle Schaller, speaks about
another kind of risk, the risk of being unprepared

for success: "If you're going to try something new, be prepared for it to work."

Risks for love are a different matter. When we love a child or a parent or a cause, we risk pain and sacrifice. We become liable to all the vulnerabilities of the person or cause we love. Yet we also share in their triumphs. What are the results of risking and working for love? The chance to reach for potential, challenging work, the chance to become a true part of our communities, relationships with people we care about and respect, the absence of in-crowds—these are what we can expect in return for true service. Since so many jobs in the for-profit world are only as big as we are, we can expect the rewards of working toward something larger than ourselves to be wonderfully surprising, sometimes beyond our imaginations. Unlike successful risks for gain, the success of risks for love simply increases our willingness to risk more—a wonderful cycle that takes us out of the boxes of the for-profit world.

Several years ago my youngest daughter had a premature child, whom I've already mentioned. There followed days of worry and apprehension as we waited to see whether the baby would survive. My daughter thought long and hard about whether to name this gift of a granddaughter, fully aware of the risk she would be taking by naming her. She decided to take the risk and named her daughter Zoe, the Greek word for *life*. Talk about a risk for love! My granddaughter survived, and the risk my daughter took in naming her was justified thousands of times over. As are most of the risks we take when we commit ourselves to the nonprofit world.

Risks seem to be welcomed and seen for what they are—opportunities to move closer to our potential—in organizations that have become movements (a subject we discussed earlier). Movements are so full of support and focus and forgiveness that risks are not unusual but only part of everyday life. In movements the absence of risk becomes a warning signal that something is not right, that the group has stumbled on its way to something it is not now.

Several ideas come to mind when I think about risks, ideas we must consider.

Risks involve ambiguity and uncertainty.

Risks result in a kind of learning available in no other way.

Risks may entail a loss of control and an acceptance of vulnerability.

Risks accompany abandoning the old, but abandoning the old makes way for the new.

Risks on the part of individuals are the only way to improve our world.

Humility invites risk; pride discourages it.

Risks are inevitable.

One last comforting thought about risk. The more we take risks, the more natural it becomes. We also learn to judge risk. I'm certain for instance that I would never be up to walking above the Grand Canyon on a tightwire. Several years ago, however, I was feeling particularly adventuresome, perhaps a bit nostalgic about my days in college following World War II when, under the GI Bill of Rights, I took flying lessons. After forty-five years I began to become interested again in the thought of flying airplanes, especially because the new planes, like the Vanguard, had a front aileron that made them easier and safer to fly.

Before starting to take lessons again I knew I would have to win Esther over to the idea. I began a careful campaign of talking from time to time about how much I had enjoyed flying and how beautiful these new airplanes were and how safe they were and how great it would be if during my retirement I could fly again. I even showed her pictures of some of these new planes from the wonderful articles in *National Geographic* and the *Smithsonian*. Finally, over a nice dinner one evening, I felt I had her all prepared, and I confessed to her what I had been thinking. I ended my presentation on a declaratory note. I said, "So, I've decided I'm going to take lessons again, get my license, and buy one of these new small airplanes." Esther looked at me for a moment, reached over, put her hand on my arm, and said, "No, you're not." Some people know how to judge risk. Take very good care of them.

And do I need to add that I'm still not flying my own airplane?

CHAPTER ELEVEN

The Function of Hope

*I*t's not hard to understand why hope was one of the seven cardinal virtues of the medieval Catholic church. Hope, faith, and charity were the three "theological" virtues; courage (fortitude), temperance, justice, and prudence were the four "natural" virtues, derived from Aristotle. Makes an interesting list for organizations, doesn't it? Without hope, it's difficult to explain existence and impossible to imagine a future. How, without hope, can you explain school to a child or the entailments of teenage pregnancy to a young woman?

How, without hope, can we in organizations expect commitment or creativity or community?

What is the organizational function of hope?

Over the years I can't recall reading in any
management or leadership books anything about
the organizational function of hope. You might
define hope as an optimistic sense of the future,
but it is also one of the most functional realities of
society. A researcher interviewed on National Public Radio not too long ago talked about teenage
pregnancy and called a "sense of the future" the
best contraceptive. It's a wonderful way to think
about hope.

A lack of hope is utterly dismal and degrading
and destructive to us personally, to us as a society. American society is rapidly realigning itself
into the hopeful and the hopeless, and tragically
the hopeless group is growing far more rapidly
than the hopeful group. We often suffer under an

enormous national myth that because so many of us are doing well, we are a well society. I wish that were true, but of course it isn't. The belief that any of us can live without hope and still be healthy is a terrible deception. In a blind and single-minded defense of individual liberties we ignore the simple fact that when a sizable minority of the members of a body is ill, the entire body is ill.

Well, what can organizations ask about the function of hope? We can begin by asking the question, Of what is hope composed? Certainly part of the answer is the ability to make choices. To be without choices is a great tragedy, a tragedy leading to hopelessness or cynicism. The ability to make choices leads to other consequences. What do we choose? How do we choose? Our choices after all set us apart and shape our legacy.

The words *volition* and *volunteer* are rooted in the Latin word *velle,* which means "to wish" or "to choose." So even the dictionary tells us that choosing and doing what we wish are related. Perhaps that's why volunteers are usually enthusiastic: they have made a choice to do something they want to do. It's no mystery why so many nonprofit organizations are filled with enthusiastic people.

Neither is it strange to think of nonprofit work and choices as related. What else does Habitat for Humanity provide—along with a new house for people who otherwise could not afford one—than choice? Doesn't Doctors Without Borders supply entire lifetimes of choice along with medical care? As a way of building hope, nonprofit organizations create choices where none existed before.

Nonprofit groups themselves must make choices. Their choices are part of personal and organizational accountability to themselves and the people they serve. Thinking of choices, of course, is another way of looking at the stands we take, the friends and enemies we keep. Our choices guide our journey. Choices are part of our stewardship of life: What shall we promise? What do we owe? What may I keep? What must I abandon? No one said choices are easy.

Making the right choices requires competence, for many choices are risky. For years a man I knew at Herman Miller had worked at the same machine, doing the same job. For thirty-five years he invariably had a cold fried-egg sandwich on white bread for lunch. I once asked him why he didn't try something else. He told me that he liked the predictability of his fried-egg sandwich and that he hated making choices. I suppose if he had been forced to eat the same thing every day, he would have felt differently about it.

Another peculiar thing about choices, we are always making them whether we do so consciously or not. It seems to me that this is one reason so many people seek out volunteer organizations: places of realized potential guide us in the choices we make, guide us to hopeful and constructive choices that contribute to a common good. People who contribute to places of realized potential have chosen to give up self-centeredness for a larger goal, for a far higher calling than individual license. If you have chosen to join a nonprofit organization and if you choose to make that group a place of realized potential, you have made the choices that are possibly the only hope for our society.

Over many years of practice and reflection I have come to see that for organizations and society in general to be civil and healthy—two wonderful criteria—leaders provide for four primary needs and rights: opportunity, identity, and equity and the design of the task.

Any hopeful person has the opportunity to work, to be involved, to be needed. Isn't it my basic right in organizations to have the opportunity to share in work, to move continually toward my potential, the opportunity to be an owner—not necessarily of equipment and property but of ideas, process, community? Challenging work adds a meaning to our lives available from nowhere else.

Identity means inclusion. If I know who I am, I know where someone has to take me in—I know where home is. Identity means to know and to be known. Identity means to be respected. Identity means to be heard. Identity means the chance to be chosen. Identity means I have a name and a place.

Some time ago I got a note from a woman who works in the finishing department of one of Herman Miller's plants and who happens to be a friend of mine. She wrote me a wonderful letter about one of the company programs that she had been through and that she thought had special value. Then came the really important part of the letter. She invited me (I happened to be chairman of the board at the time) and the board of directors to attend the next session. Her belief that to invite the board of directors to a learning session was appropriate—as it surely was—reveals a strong sense of identity.

Equity means to be fairly treated. Equity means to have access. For many years we in the United States have talked about certain gifts—the gift of talent, the gift of health, the gift of wealth. The thing we see today is that the gift of access is more important than we ever realized—access to health care, access to education, access to influence, access to justice, access to mentors who care about our future.

Equity means to be seen as authentic—not because someone works in a certain department or because of a position or promotion. We are authentic before we acquire attributes, superficial and transitory characteristics, like these. Our jobs, our organizations, our work—these are certainly important, but we have to be seen as being authentic human beings no matter what *from the beginning.* To have true equity in a community or an organization means that we are legitimate there. Equity is an essential ingredient of hope.

Designing the task is the fourth job for leaders if they are to build hope in organizations. Since nonprofits are so various in their modes of operation, the job of designing the task will involve various people, but the job has to be done. Let me propose a series of questions that seem to me to lead to well-designed tasks.

What is the unmet need or challenge facing the organization and its members? Why do we exist?

How does what we do allow both individuals
and the organization to express their
potential? We do not work in a vacuum;
neither should we labor unrewarded.

Is the task clear for individuals and the organization? Clearly communicated? What will
be measured? And when? Unmeasured
work is like an unseen painting.

Is the design of tasks both road map and treasure map? Does it give both clear direction
and room for creative contributions? A well-
designed task requires more than a manual.

Does the design of the task allow each member
of the group to answer the question, What
is *my* role? How are we connected with the
group's effort to serve a larger good?

Work in nonprofits often moves easily to competence without becoming diverted by position. I

have often asked myself why this is. The answer seems to come from the nature of the group—a movement enlists followers rather than pressing them into positions, titles, and roles. Designing the task for a movement means exposing what needs to be done, not imposing assignments on draftees. Designing the task means asking the question, How can you contribute? Then of course we must listen carefully to the answer. And in the end, designing the task means laying the foundation for hope.

I believe that hope can be thought of in terms of the obligations of leadership. Hope encourages maturity and continuity and accountability. Sadly a dearth of hope may be the most serious long-term reality in our society today. The nature of hope, of its organizational and societal role, requires us to see community as an essential condition for all. Individual liberty, highly prized in American society, exists always in relation to a common good.

In our families, in our organizations, in our society, who's going to be remembered for the gift of hope? How can each one of us become responsible for creating hope?

It seems to me that nonprofit groups are infinitely more adept at building hope than other kinds of organizations are. Through their vision, their commitment to service, their convictions concerning the common good, they have earned a distinctive position as builders of hope. Among the dozens of nonprofits each of us knows generally or in some cases intimately are models of hope-giving we can emulate. We know the local school board, the hospital, the scout troop. By their existence and their work, they give us hope for the future of our own organizational lives.

Perhaps of all the virtues hope is the most fragile, the most fleeting, the least concrete. Don't forget that the Greek gods, at the very bottom of

Pandora's box of ills and troubles, placed hope. Hope it is that allows us to cope with the rest of life. Nonprofit organizations more than any other groups in our world build hope, restore hope, exemplify hope. Nonprofit groups begin by building hope for the world and thereby build it for themselves. How can we quantify the hope created by the Peace Corps or the Red Cross or the Salvation Army? After all the money has been spent, the classes taught, the help given, the medicines distributed—isn't it hope that remains and grows?

CHAPTER TWELVE

Elements of a Legacy

*I*n searching for our potential we certainly need to distinguish between strategic planning and leaving a legacy. A strategic plan is a long-term commitment to something we intend to do. A legacy results from the facts of our behavior that remain in the minds of others, the cumulative informal record of how close we came to the person we intended to be. For me, what you plan to do differs enormously from what you leave behind.

During World War II, music seemed to reflect the reality of the times. Maybe this is true of music in all eras, but during those times it reflected an uncommon unity. It reflected a national sobriety. It spoke about unabashed love and commitment. And one particular song has stuck with me for many, many years—"Please Give Me Something to Remember You By." In fact Esther and I did most of our courting by mail for three years during World War II. So to us the idea of giving somebody else something to remember you by is a very real thought.

For me, it is also a very real thought for organizations and the people who lead them. This idea lies at the heart of the concept of a legacy, both personally and organizationally. Over the years and upon much reflection I've come to believe that realizing our potential requires us to think purposefully about a legacy.

What will I give you to remember me by is a question for each of us as we think about the people we work with, the people who love us, the people who need us. I believe this a gift worth pondering. What will I give you to remember me by?

How can we think about the idea of a legacy? How can we examine this idea and then develop a guiding attitude about it? Thinking about a legacy is not as straightforward as setting goals and measuring results. A legacy, it seems to me, has a deeper and more enduring and more substantial place in the lives of organizations than meeting goals.

People we admire decide who they intend to be, because what we do will always be a consequence of who we have become. It's much easier to sit down and define a problem than to ruminate on what we want to become. But no one would argue that planning a life takes precedence over setting tomorrow's agenda. How we live our lives and how we think about our work give us an idea of what kind of legacy we may leave. As I think about the idea of a legacy, there's a wonderful and mysterious sense in which our legacy is our name.

I would like to suggest several additional elements to a legacy. You'll have others, but this is a beginning list.

I believe that when we're trying to establish a legacy, we try to become competent in establishing and maintaining relationships. The longer I live and the more I see of organizations, the more I'm forced to the conclusion that at the heart of our organizations is always this matter of competence in relationships. This, I believe, is the second level of quality (the first is truth). While technical skill and lifetime learning are essential, I'm convinced that competence in relationships remains most important in making organizations places of realized potential. Even though many people in the United States expend only words in the pursuit of quality, many others are seriously interested in realizing the idea.

Learning competence in relationships comes from family, friends, mentors, idols. It results from observation, conscious and unconscious. It derives from selflessness and real concern and our beliefs about people. It results in civility, love, and devotion to a common good. Nothing guarantees it; no one succeeds without it.

A true legacy establishes a direction. It always suggests a vision, something very different from a strategy. People write down a strategy and follow it. We *see* a vision and *pursue* it. A clear sense of direction is the necessary foundation for a life of service. When I think of true legacy leavers—Mohandas Gandhi or Albert Schweitzer—I immediately think of the directions their lives followed. There is no mistaking their direction and commitment to it.

Fending for the truth can become a legacy. If you listen to government leaders, if you read and listen to corporate advertising, if you're a penetrating reader of the media, you'll see that our society is becoming callous toward truth. It's true that as we become more diverse and more disparate, truth is less and less obvious. Universal truths still exist, just as surely as they did in the past. Truth has to be our first level of quality. Without truth we react in a temporary way to daily pressures. A legacy helps others preserve and illuminate the truth. Truth can become part of our legacy only if we live it. We should also remember that truth is truth, even if spoken by Balaam's ass.

In building a legacy we choose to be personally accountable. There are many circumstances in life that hold no choices for us, but one of the choices we can make is to be personally accountable. We can accept responsibility for our own actions. We accept responsibility for our own lifetime learning program, and we can choose not to deprive others of a level of accountability that for most of us is natural. I've always found it telling that in the face of major mistakes, members of the British cabinet resign as a way of saying publicly "I'm responsible. I'll pay the price for my actions."

A legacy sets standards. I find it interesting that in my experience at Herman Miller, the company observed standards that in many cases were more than forty years old, very different from dealing with the standards and structures of a three-year plan or a five-year plan or any kind of a strategy. It seems to me that we spend far more time in organizations living up to standards than setting them. The legacies people leave over time

to organizations and to communities and to families set standards that last far longer than ones set
by committees. They are standards not just of performance but of dignity and servanthood, of good
manners, good taste, and decorum. Our society
cries out for the civility that results from high
standards.

Guiding legacies lift the spirit. We all have a
right to a spirit-lifting presence in our leaders, and
such a presence can become a legacy. This is
something to be remembered by. If we can be a
spirit-lifting presence among those with whom we
work, we have begun to understand inspiration.

*A person building a legacy is the exemplar of
what I call "more than meets the eye."* I think
most of us are familiar with the kind of person I'm
describing. A simple question will illustrate what I
mean. Given the choice, would you rather be
someone about whom people say, "There's more

to her than meets the eye" or "There's less to her than meets the eye"? The kind of person I'm talking about is at ease with personal restraint and at the same time knows the organizational importance of constraints. Capacity does not mandate use. The most powerful people I know wield their power carefully.

A person building a legacy welcomes constructive constraints and seeks simplicity as an essential condition of life. In my work life I've had the wonderful opportunity to work with a great many creative people, all of whom talk about the importance of understanding constraints. Constraints for truly creative people are never a problem but an opportunity and a guide.

People trying to build a legacy will make sure that their own houses are in order. George Kennan, who had a long history in the U.S. State Department, wrote the original paper for the American government on dealing with the USSR following the end of World War II. Kennan is a wise, philosophical, experienced State Department hand. In the course of an interview somebody asked him what our foreign policy should be during the Clinton administration. He thought for a minute and said that the best foreign policy the United States can have is to get its own house in order. I think this is a wonderful, personal admonition for those wanting to leave a legacy and for those wishing to become leaders.

People thinking about their legacies strive to integrate their lives upward. This is an interesting idea for me. In our work how uplifting this idea of integrating upward can be! For instance we want to bring our work up to the standards of our beliefs. We integrate our work up to the level of our faith. We want to make our relationships—the quality of our relationships—consistent with what we believe about persons. I often wonder what we as a society could do with the problem of teenage pregnancies if we thought about raising passion up to love rather than defining love in terms of passion. What could we achieve in our schools and churches and universities if we sought out a more *un*common denominator?

A legacy lives in the actions of many people. One of the people who taught me a great deal was Charles Eames, a famous industrial designer who worked with Herman Miller for years. Someone once said about Charles that when you worked with him you were always learning but he was never teaching. That's a wonderful thought in itself. The idea of unconscious mentoring is part of Charles's legacy and has taken shape in the behavior of many people at the company today. A good friend of mine, a writer at the company, often repeats this observation though he never met Eames!

While working with Charles one day in his Venice, California, studio, I heard him say that his wife, Ray, was celebrating her birthday today and that we would be having dinner at their home that evening. "On our way home," he said, "let's plan to pick up some flowers." Somewhat naively I thought he meant a stop at a florist's shop to pick up a prearranged bouquet. How wrong I was. We drove to the old farmer's market, where Charles over the course of two hours carefully picked out every single flower for the bouquet, all of the accompanying greens, and the ribbon and wrapping paper. While he had not set out to teach me something, I confess it was a wonderful learning experience for me. It taught me a lot about the giving of gifts and the importance of celebrations.

Each of us is capable of being a mentor in one way or another. If we think about leaving a legacy, we will establish these relationships, because mentoring is a really crucial element to growth. A million mentors wouldn't be too many!

Finally, a legacy is the most significant way of saying thank you to an organization and the people with whom you work. Work can be one of the most health-giving parts of our lives, and life in organizations is often a part of work. We all know of people whose work becomes an expression of gratitude for the chance to contribute. Frank Lloyd Wright used to speak of the houses he designed as a way of thanking individuals and society for the freedom to use his talent. What we leave behind, more than anything else we can do or say, tells the world what we thought of an organization and its work.

One last thought about legacies. In one sense everybody leaves a legacy, even though that legacy may be only a blip on the roster of volunteers. A legacy may consist of words, a building, a single deed. One powerful moment may be our legacy, and we may not even realize it at the time. I don't think Rosa Parks thought about the wonderful legacy she was leaving us when she refused to give up her seat on the bus to a white man. Was Anthony McAuliffe thinking about his legacy when he said, "Nuts!" to the surrounding German army at Bastogne in the Battle of the Bulge? I think these people were simply doing what they thought was right. And they were prepared to act on their beliefs.

What seems crucial to me is that we think consciously about what kind of legacy we want to leave our organizations, our communities, our families. Are we ready for that moment when our convictions will be tested? Have we considered what the building we are erecting will mean decades from now? Have we thought what our actions and decisions *now* will mean to our organization years from now? Once we begin to think in terms of our legacy, what a different light suffuses everything about our lives and our work!

CHAPTER THIRTEEN

Moral Purpose
and Active Virtue

Without moral purpose, competence has no measure and trust no goal. This defining thought gives me a way to think about the place of moral purpose in our organizations.

In every church and monastery in Celtic Britain and Ireland a fire was kept burning as a sign of God's presence. This is the way I as a Christian see moral purpose—as a sign of God's presence in our organizations. It's up to us to keep the signs of moral purpose alive and visible in organizations. In vital organizations, those groups whose purpose has both pragmatic and moral dimensions, people reach outward to serve others and inward toward their own potential. Surely potential cannot be thought of only in financial or material terms. Let me propose five signs of moral purpose I've seen over the years.

The first sign of what I call God's presence is a wholehearted acceptance of human authenticity. We are all authentic. We are not authentic because we have been hired by a company or because we have been admitted as a student to a particular college or because we have married a particular man or woman. We are not authentic because of government programs spelling out the rules for hiring minorities or people with disabilities. As parts of a great cross-cultural society, we form a cornucopia of gifts and talents. We are genuinely insiders in this world because we are God's mix—we are made in his image.

Authenticity needs to dominate our relationships and our understanding of justice. The implications of this belief are enormous.

Second, because we are authentic, we are entitled to certain rights as insiders: the right to belong, the right to ownership, the right to opportunity, the right to a covenantal relationship, the right to inclusive organizations.   Groups with a clear moral purpose work to make these rights real, led by people who understand the strength inherent in working toward something outside of, and larger than, themselves.

Third, leaders in groups with a clear moral purpose make themselves vulnerable—a gift of all true leaders to their followers.   Moral purpose enables leaders to be vulnerable because it changes the rules of measurement. A clear moral purpose removes the ego from the game. It means that leaders no longer need to succeed on the terms that make some leaders intolerant, inaccessible, and insufferable. Vulnerable leaders are open to the diversity of gifts from followers. They seek contrary opinion. They take every person seriously. They are strong enough to abandon themselves to the strengths of others.

Fourth, groups with a clear moral purpose to their actions take very seriously realistic and equitable distribution of results. I'm talking about distributing the normal results of nonprofit institutions—challenging and rewarding work, meaningful personal growth, service to others. What is fair and motivating to authentic insiders from whom leaders demand a meaningful contribution? As 1 Corinthians reminds us: "Who plants a vineyard without eating any of its fruit? Who tends a flock without getting some of the milk?" Who, indeed?

An example from the for-profit world: at Herman Miller the board limited the cash compensation of the CEO to twenty times the average compensation of employees. The company had for many years productivity gain sharing in cash bonuses and paid out profit sharing quarterly in fully negotiable Herman Miller stock. These practices didn't happen accidentally. They were all attempts to distribute the results of our work equitably. Of course not all results are tangible. And not all compensation consists of money or stock. Nonprofit groups have to work especially hard at finding inventive and effective ways of distributing results.

The equitable distribution of results may be the most convincing evidence of a leader and a group clearly guided in their jobs by moral purpose.

The fifth sign of God's presence I'd like to suggest is personal restraint. Leaders, especially leaders of nonprofit groups, work in public, under constant scrutiny. We may not like that—in fact I often resented the intrusions that came with my job as CEO—but that's reality. Since leaders function in public, perceptions of leaders are crucial to their performance. It seems to me that this also holds true for nonprofit groups. They can express what's best in our culture, including restraint—the belief that personal gain falls far down on the list of important achievements in one's life.

It also seems to me that a clear moral purpose to life and work results in active virtue. Now I'm aware that cloistered virtue can also be admirable, but in the world of organizations, both nonprofit and for-profit, actions must follow words.

Leaders in nonprofit groups—and you'll remember that I think leadership is a job, not a title—have special questions about active virtue. What message does a leader's way of living send to people about what she thinks is right, who matters, and what moves followers? What signals do leaders send with their power, their status, and their privileges? Nothing is more dispiriting than the discovery of a leader in a vital organization who has betrayed the moral purpose of the group to obtain a few paltry signs of personal power and wealth. Evidence of this tragedy shows up all too regularly.

What is the real purpose of talent and wealth? Surely they are gifts to us, but are those gifts only for our use? How can we share equitably, and how are we to employ for the common good the unearned gift of access? Access—to resources, education, or opportunity for example—is a gift, like talent or wealth, that exacts accountability.

How in the context of a world of limited resources are we to understand and practice simplicity?

How are we to distinguish between individual liberty and license, to modulate our liberty in light of the common good? A poem by theologian Walter Wietzke interprets God's message to us in this regard: "I have not called you to license, for in that error society and selfhood is lost. / I have called you to liberty, for in its truthful tension, society and selfhood is found." (Carl Frost quotes the full poem in his recent book, *Changing Forever.*)

I certainly don't have the answers to all of the questions I've posed to you, but I do think that, as each of us deals seriously with them, we will come to understand how a moral purpose can guide our work. Without a moral purpose, we sail along rudderless, coping with the inevitable wind and waves but making little progress toward the destinations we pick for ourselves.

Epilogue

*I*n the seemingly hopeless summer of 1941, as the German army approached Leningrad (now back to its original name of St. Petersburg), the staff of the Hermitage Museum packed up tens of thousands of paintings and sculptures, antiquities and treasures, to be shipped east, away from the Germans and the upcoming siege. It was a tragic time.

The staff left the empty frames and pedestals in their proper places in the museum as a sign of their conviction that someday they would be able to restore the Hermitage and its priceless collection of art. Though they were losing their art, they were determined not to lose hope.

The Germans surrounded Leningrad for more than two years, and the Russians endured that long and arduous time with little to eat and often under attack. The staff of the Hermitage and their families moved into the basement of the museum, determined to preserve the building. Russian soldiers and citizens came regularly to help clean up the damage done by the German artillery and to patch up as best they could the broken windows to keep out the snow. As a way of saying thank you, the staff conducted tours of the museum for these people. But of course the art wasn't there.

Photographs show the Hermitage curators conducting the tours, avoiding the piles of snow on the beautiful parquet floors, with the groups of soldiers standing in front of empty picture frames and forlorn pedestals. The curators described from memory and in great detail the Renoirs and the Rembrandts to the soldiers, filling in the blank

spaces in their wonderful museum with their own dedication, commitment, and love.

This, to me, is a picture of service and hope. This, to me, is what it means to see one's potential and to move doggedly toward it.

The Author

*M*ax De Pree writes from forty years of experience in the corporate world, almost that many in the nonprofit world, and nineteen years as a grandparent. De Pree is chairman emeritus of Herman Miller, Inc., a member of *Fortune* magazine's National Business Hall of Fame, and a recipient of the Business Enterprise Trust's Lifetime Achievement Award, and he has served on the boards of Fuller Theological Seminary, Hope College, and Words of Hope. He is also a member of the advisory board of the Peter F. Drucker Foundation for Nonprofit Management. He has seen hope in his service to a variety of communities.

De Pree is the author of three books: *Leadership Is an Art* (1987), *Leadership Jazz* (1992), and *Dear Zoe* (1994).

De Pree and his wife, Esther, have four children and eleven grandchildren.

Please remember that this is a library book, and that it belongs only temporarily to each person who uses it. Be considerate. Do not write in this, or any, library book.

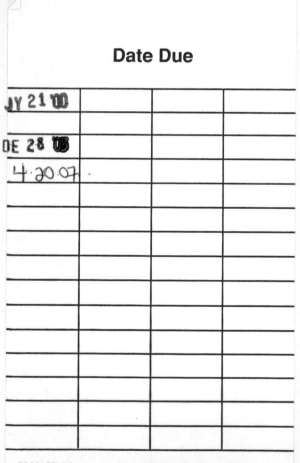

Date Due

JY 21 '00			
DE 28 '03			
4·20·07 ·			